Advance Praise for *The Milk Memos*

"Child development experts have long recommended to business leaders that they can increase worker productivity and tenure by creating family-friendly workplaces. The tension between trying to be both a competent parent and an effective employee comes to life in *The Milk Memos*, based on exchanges among working mothers that touch both the heart and mind. These women make their problems palpable and ultimately convey what supports they need to balance work and family life. A must-read for both parents and employers."

—EDWARD ZIGLER, PH.D., Sterling Professor of Psychology emeritus, Yale University

"In twelve years of working with breastfeeding mothers and their babies, I've never come across a more balanced, practical, and funny how-to guide on managing the dance of working and breastfeeding."

—AMANDA OGDEN, RN, BSN, international board-certified lactation consultant

"Being a new, nursing mommy is a big enough challenge. But combine that with working full-time and pumping breast milk several times a day in a janitor's closet, bathroom stall, or cubicle, and it's enough to make a postpartum mom cry more than she's already crying. *The Milk Memos* gives comfort and advice to moms at a time when they need it most. It's a must read for any new stay-at-work mommy who's toting a breast pump along with her briefcase."

—WENDY SACHS, author of *How She Really Does It: Secrets of Successful Stay-at-Work Moms*

• • •

JEREMY P. TARCHER/PENGUIN

a member of Penguin Group (USA) Inc.

New York

the milk memos

HOW REAL MOMS LEARNED

TO MIX BUSINESS WITH BABIES—

AND HOW YOU CAN, TOO

cate colburn-smith

and

andrea serrette

JEREMY P. TARCHER/PENGUIN
Published by the Penguin Group
Penguin Group (USA) Inc., 375 Hudson Street, New York, New York 10014, USA •
Penguin Group (Canada), 90 Eglinton Avenue East, Suite 700, Toronto, Ontario M4P 2Y3, Canada
(a division of Pearson Penguin Canada Inc.) • Penguin Books Ltd, 80 Strand,
London WC2R 0RL, England • Penguin Ireland, 25 St Stephen's Green, Dublin 2, Ireland
(a division of Penguin Books Ltd) • Penguin Group (Australia), 250 Camberwell Road,
Camberwell, Victoria 3124, Australia (a division of Pearson Australia Group Pty Ltd) •
Penguin Books India Pvt Ltd, 11 Community Centre, Panchsheel Park, New Delhi–110 017, India •
Penguin Group (NZ), 67 Apollo Drive, Mairangi Bay, Auckland 1311,
New Zealand (a division of Pearson New Zealand Ltd) • Penguin Books (South Africa) (Pty) Ltd,
24 Sturdee Avenue, Rosebank, Johannesburg 2196, South Africa

Penguin Books Ltd, Registered Offices: 80 Strand, London WC2R 0RL, England

Most Tarcher/Penguin books are available at special quantity discounts for bulk purchase for sales promotions, premiums, fund-raising, and educational needs. Special books or book excerpts also can be created to fit specific needs. For details, write Penguin Group (USA) Inc. Special Markets, 375 Hudson Street,
New York, NY 10014.

Library of Congress Cataloging-in-Publication Data

Colburn-Smith, Cate, date.
The milk memos : how real moms learned to mix business with babies—
and how you can, too / Cate Colburn-Smith and Andrea Serrette.
p.   cm.
Includes index.
ISBN 978-1-58542-544-0
1. Working mothers—Life skills guides.   2. Working mothers—United States—Diaries.
3. Infants—Care.   4. Mother and infant.   I. Serrette, Andrea, date.   II. Title.
HQ759.48.C64   2007   2006037107
306.874'30973—dc22

Printed in the United States of America
1   3   5   7   9   10   8   6   4   2

BOOK DESIGN BY MEIGHAN CAVANAUGH

For Caleb, Charlotte, and Mary

. . . and Milk Mamas everywhere

contents

the milk memos

introduction

Our paths first crossed in a crowded IBM conference room, Cate's belly ready to burst under her black maternity sweater, Andrea not yet aware that she, too, was pregnant. Pens poised for note taking, we sat across from each other at the giant brown conference table, both of us less than riveted by the meeting subject at hand: how to reenergize the IBM sales force. From the outside looking in, everything about this meeting was business as usual. But for us, that day was the beginning of something extraordinary. Without even realizing it, we were drawn together as soon-to-be moms in the deadline-driven, high-tech, fast-paced culture of corporate America. Neither of us could have imagined how powerful our bond as moms would be, nor how essential our pens and notebooks would become to our survival at work.

Almost a year later, we met again, this time toting breastpumps and looking for ways to reenergize ourselves. Cate was nearing the end of her year-long pumping career, and Andrea was just beginning hers. We ran into each other as Cate was coming out of the IBM lactation room, a small janitor's closet inside the women's restroom. It was Andrea's first day back. Still puffy-eyed and choked up after leaving her son, Caleb, Andrea couldn't hold back her tears. Without speaking, Cate gave her a hug that said, *Sister, I know what you're going through.*

After several minutes of reassuring hugs in between crying and dabbing our eyes with tissues, Cate told Andrea to read the two spiral notebooks sitting on the brown table in the lactation room and asked her to call any time she needed to talk.

Andrea finally entered the lactation room and shut the door behind her, all alone for her initiation to pumping at work. She pulled her shirt up and bra down, and turned on her pump. As milk slowly dripped into the bottles, Andrea looked at the baby pictures taped to the beige cinder-block walls and wondered, *How do other moms do this day after day?*

The answer was in the pages of the notebooks, where we swapped baby stories and tips, and mused about how to successfully blend career and motherhood. We shared personal details about everything from postpartum periods to spontaneous breastmilk squirting during sex, and we hashed over the challenges of finding good day care, getting a decent night's sleep, and taking a 6:00 A.M. conference call while trying to soothe a crying baby.

"MOMMY LOVES YOU"

For those of us who work outside of the home, either by choice or necessity, the day comes when we must kiss our babies good-bye. How do we do it? We walk away armed with our breastpumps, blinking away the tears, and we try to be brave. We tell ourselves our babies will be well taken care of. We tell ourselves the work we do is worthwhile, and that we are providing for our families. At one level, we are relieved to have a break from the all-consuming demands of full-time motherhood. We find pleasure in the relationships, the mental stimulation, and the challenges we face at work.

At a deeper level, we feel guilty. We know that no one can truly substitute for mommy. No one can ever know or love our children as we do. And underlying the guilt, we feel the longing. It's like the longing of new romantic love, only a thousand times stronger. So intense that we can't think about it too long, for fear that our hearts will break and our resolve crumble.

Somehow, miraculously, we make it through those first days and weeks without collapsing. We lift each other up. And slowly but surely, we all become stronger, and increasingly capable of achieving a workable balance between our careers and our babies. Trust us—you'll get there, too.

We are thoroughly convinced that you don't have to choose between having a career and being a great mom. We do both—and so can you. Be confident in the value you bring to work *and* in your natural ability to love and nurture your child. The fact that you're returning to work in the first place demonstrates a commitment to your career. Pumping at work can be your stake in the ground from the beginning that says, "I'm a mom, first and foremost." By doing this, you will also keep providing your baby with the ultimate sustenance for him, and you'll remain intimately connected with him in a way only you can be.

MILK!

As you will soon learn, much of our conversation in the notebooks was dedicated to the ups and downs, and the art and science of pumping breastmilk at work. Our milk obsession stemmed from the fact that we were all committed to breastfeeding our babies, which meant pumping at work, no matter how challenging and inconvenient it was. Plus, we were constantly aware of our breasts, which had taken on a life of their own. Gone was the luxury of only thinking about them when we needed a push-up bra for perkiness and cleavage under a little black dress. Now, we and our babies relied on these appendages to produce, store, and deliver breastmilk. On top of taking care of our newborns, we also had to take care of our breasts!

We came to learn that, compared to other moms who worked outside the home, we had a pretty good setup at IBM: a private place to pump, and some semblance of a lactation program. Most of our friends worked for companies that didn't provide such "luxuries." There are countless moms (especially in noncorporate settings) who pump on open toilet seats in public bathroom stalls. Or in the back corner of a retail inventory room. Or in a parked car during a snowstorm. They pumped in a cubicle with a makeshift curtain for privacy. Or in a conference room with a broken lock. Or in a parked car during a snowstorm. To make matters worse, some of these moms were then reprimanded for being away too often for their pumping "breaks."

 breastfeeding legislation

- Your right to breastfeed and/or pump at work is essentially protected under the Pregnancy Discrimination Act, an amendment made in 1978 to Title VII of the Civil Rights Act of 1964.

The act prohibits employers with fifteen or more employees, including state and local governments, from discriminating against you because of pregnancy, childbirth, or *related medical conditions*. It is enforced via the U.S. Equal Employment Opportunity Commission.

- The Breastfeeding Promotion Act, currently being considered by Congress, would amend Title VII to specifically protect *breastfeeding*. It would also provide tax incentives for businesses that establish private lactation areas in the workplace, a performance standard for breastpumps, and a tax deduction on breastfeeding equipment for families.

- To bolster the federal support, currently thirty-one states have specific laws covering the rights of mothers to breastfeed in any public or private location, and twelve states have laws related to breastfeeding in the workplace.

Because our friends didn't have adequate lactation support at work, it's no wonder many of them gave up breastfeeding not long after their maternity leaves ended. Even with support, we found that pumping at work was much more complicated (yet more gratifying) than we ever expected. Beyond our company's backing, we needed one another's help and encouragement to keep going. The notebooks became our sounding board, our venting ground, our FAQ resource, and our cheering squad.

So, all this said, we'll point out upfront that this book is chock-full of breastfeeding information and tips. In large part, this is a matter of first things first. From the time your baby latches on to your breast in her first few moments of life, your breastmilk and the act of nursing her are some of the most fundamental and life-sustaining gifts you can offer. Finding a way to keep this connection alive after you return to work, despite the fact that you're away from your baby for a big chunk of the day, can be amazingly comforting for both of you. It's also one of the best things you can do to maintain your baby's health. The benefits of breastfeeding are widely documented and extolled—diverse and compelling, immediate and long term, physical, emotional, and cognitive, for infants as well as mothers. Our milk does everything from boosting our babies' immune systems to raising their IQs, while simultaneously decreasing our risk of breast cancer, and helping us relax and stay connected with our babies. Why give this up? And if you manage to continue breastfeeding (and pumping) upon your return to work (we *know* you can!), you're off to a great start in navigating the waters of working motherhood.

The other reason breasts and milk figure so prominently throughout this book is, well, for one thing, we were pumping while we wrote! But more than this, it feels to us that there is something about it—being at work behind a locked door, breasts exposed, pumping breastmilk while reading e-mails, listening to a conference call, and two minutes later being totally composed and dashing into a meeting—that is really a metaphor for the whole experience of working motherhood. It just doesn't get more tangible than that!

BEAT THE ODDS

If you're considering breastfeeding while working outside the home, you're in good company—breastfeeding rates are at record highs in the United States. And half of all mothers return to work during their child's first year of life, when breastfeeding is so important. Unfortunately, though more and more working moms intend to continue breastfeeding, most give up within three months. In fact, returning to work is the number-one reason moms quit nursing. Take a mom away from her baby, add sleep deprivation, stress from all directions, constant worry about milk supply, and the inevitable mishap of a forgotten pump part or spilled milk, and there are bound to be days when that mom is ready to dropkick her breastpump down the stairwell and check into a spa.

Not surprisingly, stay-at-home moms breastfeed at significantly higher rates, and for longer durations, than moms who work outside the home. Both groups initiate breast-

Comparison of Breastfeeding Rates

	EARLY POSTPARTUM	AT 6 MONTHS	AT 12 MONTHS
Full-time Working Moms	68%	23%	11%
Part-time Working Moms	68%	33%	19%
Stay-at-home Moms	68%	35%	22%
Healthy People 2010 Goals*	75%	50%	25%

Source: American Academy of Family Physicians
*Healthy People 2010 goals were established by the United States Department of Health and Human Services in 2000.

feeding at the same rate, but this rate declines sharply for moms who return to work.

HOW THIS BOOK WILL HELP YOU

Our little stack of tattered lactation-room notebooks provided much-needed solace and powerful inspiration—about

breastfeeding and so much more. The notebooks helped us
feel less alone. Friendships formed quickly, and eventually
we began looking forward to pumping and keeping abreast
(ha) of the "news." We supported and encouraged each
other as we trudged through each day, somehow managing
to keep a sense of humor about it all.

It wasn't long before we discovered that we had more
in common than being breastfeeding, working moms. We
shared a dream to turn the notebooks into a book. We
thought if our little circle of moms found the notebooks to
be so helpful, surely others would, too. That's how the idea
for *The Milk Memos* was born, and with it, our fervent hope
that we could support and inspire other working mothers to
persevere, especially as they faced the enormous challenge
of returning to the workforce after maternity leave.

We hope and pray that this book will reach all kinds of
moms, especially those who feel unsure and alone, and don't
have the direct support of other new working moms with
whom to share the whole crazy experience. You will find
practical advice about pumping: how to select a pump, how
to prepare for returning to work, how much milk your baby
needs, how to increase your supply, how to relieve a clogged
duct, how to camouflage wet breastmilk circles on your shirt,
how long pumped milk can be stored, how to carry it back

from a business trip, whether to supplement with formula, and when and how to wean. Beyond this, you will find guidance and reassurance on the subjects most trying for working moms, such as coming to terms with leaving your precious baby in the care of another, coping with clueless managers or coworkers who find your pumping annoying, and trying to perform your work as well as you did prebaby, despite the fact that you're sleep deprived, you've now got two full-time jobs, and your new little boss is extremely demanding.

Everything you're about to read was inspired by the original lactation-room notebooks and happened to real working, nursing moms—some who pumped with us at IBM, and many others who shared their stories as we wrote the book. These Milk Mamas (as we began to call ourselves) ranged from the very career driven to the very baby centered and in between; from single moms, moms in traditional married households, and moms in blended families (with children from previous marriages); from first-time moms to seasoned veteran moms; from moms who relished breastfeeding to moms who dutifully endured it out of sheer love for their babies. Though diverse, we were united by our common commitment and dedication to nursing our babies. For a few moments once or twice a day, we stepped into our little lactation room and poured out our hearts while emptying our breasts. We tuned into and revealed our true, most motherly mammal selves. Sharing our breastfeeding, pumping, and mothering thoughts and questions enabled us to cope, and sometimes even thrive, in the gender-neutral world of business, and alas, paychecks.

Here is our story. We hope it makes yours a little easier.

prologue

CATE'S FIRST DAY

Tired, lonely, sad, I sat at a brown medical examination table as if it were a desk, yellowing paper gowns still in the drawers, a relic from when IBM had an on-site medical facility. Staring at a blank wall, I tried to let the hum of the fluorescent lights and my breastpump motor hypnotize me. Far from cozy, this tiny lactation room was at least private. Drip, drip, drip. All alone, ever so slowly, I filled little plastic bottles with precious breastmilk for my baby girl, who might as well have been a million miles away.

It was my first day back at work following a four-month maternity leave. My heart ached as I finally allowed the tears to flow freely. *This is* so *depressing compared to actually nursing Charlotte,* I thought. I imagined her little hands holding my breast, her warm, sweet mouth suckling, her little jaw moving in rhythm, her eyes half-closed, her whole being in perfect harmony with mine.

I am one of those moms who *loves* nursing. I am continually amazed at how Mother Nature so perfectly designed mother and baby for it. I'll never forget how, in Charlotte's first moments of life, so perfect and tiny, her mouth found my breast and she knew instinctively how to nurse. I was blessed with an easy pregnancy, and I *loved* the joyful anticipation and feminine grace of it. For me breastfeeding is the next best thing to pregnancy: motherhood in its purest form, a connection unique and beautiful, a rare chance to experience bliss.

As I pumped that first day, I imagined mothers and babies all over the globe nursing. Women in indigenous cultures in far-flung parts of the world. Women in my neighborhood. Career women—CEOs, senators. Everyday women. Someone somewhere in the middle of the night, half-asleep, gently picking up her infant and holding her for a moment against her chest, smelling her, slowly swaying back and forth, and sitting down to nurse her by the soft glow of a nightlight.

I prayed that continuing to breastfeed Charlotte while working outside the home would be my saving grace. I needed to remain connected to Charlotte both physically and emotionally as I provided her with (this sounds bold, but it's true) the source of life itself. *Only* I could provide breastmilk. Sweet, delicious (go ahead, try a drop!), and nutritionally perfect.

I longed for the comfort, understanding, and companionship of other new, breastfeeding, working mothers. How else could I survive the difficult transition back to work?

The Milk Memos began when I scribbled this on a paper towel:

Monday, March 12

I'm a new mom and today is my first day back at work. Is anyone else using this room?

Cate

ONE

. . .

first day back

Monday, March 12

Welcome, Cate!

How are you doing on your first day back? I will bring in an extra box of tissues for you—I know how hard the first couple weeks are. How old is your baby? I'm nursing my second son, George, who just turned 2 months. I came back to work when he was 6 weeks old, which was way too soon, but I didn't really have a choice. My husband, Bill, left Sun to make his fortunes with a start-up software company which is still struggling to make payroll, but has "HUGE" potential. Needless to say, we need my income and benefits.

Our older son, Colby, is 2. This lactation room wasn't here when I was pumping for him. I was a squatter—one day I would pump in my manager's office, the next in a conference room, then at my desk while my office mate was out to lunch, and a few times in the fitness center laundry room (seemed like a good idea until the heat of the dryer had me sweating as hard as the people in spin class—and burning just as many calories—ha!). This lactation room is not exactly inviting, but we really are lucky to have it.

Well, I'm off to a meeting. Write back and tell me all about your baby!

Stacy

Tuesday, March 13

Stacy,

It's so nice to "meet" you! I brought in this spiral notebook thinking I'd be writing to myself. I thought maybe if I let my emotions flow in here I could hold myself together in meetings. It's so great to actually talk to another working, nursing mom. These first two days have been almost unbearable. My daughter, Charlotte, is going on 4 months old, and until yesterday I had never been away from her for longer than *three hours*! She loves to play with her feet, and she is on the verge of rolling over. I feel like I'm missing everything.

Cate

P.S. Feel free to write back in this notebook. We could become pumping pen pals!

Tuesday, March 13

Cate,

This notebook is a great idea!

I hear you—it is so hard to come back to work after maternity leave. I'm barely able to sit down without my hospital-issued whoopee cushion (did I mention George was 9lbs, 1oz?!), and now I have to sit on my butt all day long designing Web pages.

Even the second time around, and even though I'm "one of those moms" who truly enjoys my career, I am struggling with being back here. I miss George's smiles and coos and Colby's hugs and kisses. It does get better (believe it or not). But for now, if misery loves company, we'll make great pumping pals. Your new friend,

Stacy

P.S. I don't think anyone else is using this room. Weird. Maybe we're the only ones who know about it?

BACK-TO-WORK BLUES

Milk Mamas, we're going to tell it to you straight. Your first day back will be miserable. Whether you're looking forward to returning to work or dreading it, your maternity leave will end too quickly. The thought of leaving your baby in the care of another while you go off to face customers, meetings, e-mails, conference calls, and deadlines—never mind getting yourself showered, dressed, and out the door by 8:00 A.M.—is daunting . . . but inevitable.

Other Milk Mamas have gone before you. Like you, we cried. We called our moms, sisters, and girlfriends. We knew the day would come, but somehow hoped it wouldn't. Our husbands tried to reassure us, but they couldn't. Nobody could. Truly, we grieved. We knew our babies would never be this tiny again. We would never be able to reclaim the hours spent away from them. Someone else would now be holding them, soothing them, kissing them. How is it that maternity leave, so foreign at first, turned out to be so comfortable? The days passed slowly but the weeks sped by in a dizzying blur.

In hindsight, maternity leave was boot camp and bliss all wrapped up in one. One day we were polished and professional, entertaining clients, preparing a presentation or traveling across the globe. The next day we were bleary-eyed, changing soupy diapers, wearing spit-up-stained PJs, and feeling overwhelmed by tasks as simple as unloading the dishwasher or brushing our teeth. Ah, but we were with our babies—the most beautiful, perfect, tiny angels ever to grace the planet—right there in our arms! We quickly learned to love the hours upon hours of just *being* with our little cherubs, staring at them, nursing them, mothering them. Have you ever met a mom who didn't treasure her maternity leave? We haven't. Which brings us back to our first point. Day one back at work sneaks up on you like your thirtieth birthday, only there's no party.

Instead, there's a parade of well-meaning colleagues welcoming you back and asking endless questions about your baby, which just makes you miss him all the more. Besides giving the baby report, you'll spend the day trying to refocus your mind on your work, and figuring out when and how to pump. You will count the hours until you can be with your baby again. And you will probably cry.

Wednesday, March 14

I wonder if Charlotte misses me as much as I miss her. I can't stop thinking about her. I can't concentrate at all on work—partly because I'm so tired, but mostly because I'm having a hard time switching from being a full-time mom and the center of Charlotte's universe to sitting in meetings, answering e-mails, and writing a new strategy document. It seems like a month ago, but only last Friday I was relaxing in my leather recliner watching Ellen DeGeneres while Charlotte nursed and fell asleep at my breast. I hate to be glass-half-empty, but is it really *only* Wednesday? I've been crying every morning on the way to work. *I hate this*. WHEN does it get easier?

Cate

Wednesday, March 14

Oh Cate,

I want to give you a big hug. I know you don't believe me, but I can tell you from experience that it will get easier in a month or two. Remember breaking up with your first love? You were sure you would never get over it. But the sun continued to rise and set, and as the days and weeks passed, you did recover. And you emerged stronger than before. Thank God we're not breaking up with our babies. But it can feel that way . . . because we miss them so much, and because the relationship is changing and won't ever be the same. I'm making myself cry now! As I said, I'm actually one of those working moms who can't imagine being home. I love my career and my independence, yet I still feel sad— some days more than others. Regardless of how into your career you are, the first week is the worst. Hang in there.

Stacy

Wednesday, March 14

Thanks, Stacy.

My one consolation is that Charlotte is home with my husband, Chris, 2½ days a week, and with a nanny the other 2½ days. Chris works for IBM too, and he went part-time when I came back from maternity leave because we couldn't bear the thought of Charlotte spending 5 days/week with a stranger. Since my income is much higher than Chris's, we decided I would be the one to work full-time. It's so strange that after working *so hard* to get where I am, I sort of wish I made less money so I wouldn't "have" to be the primary, full-time breadwinner. I never expected it to be this hard.

Cate

TIME HEALS

Some Milk Mamas cry on the way to work every morning for weeks. Others adjust more quickly, and some—dare they admit—are actually relieved to get back to work. They miss maternity leave as much as any other mom, but know that full-time motherhood is not their calling. The truth is, the experience is different for everyone. There are no step-by-step guides for getting through the first few weeks. You will naturally find the routine that's right for you. Leaving home and pumping at work is uncomfortable and foreign at first, but you'll be surprised how quickly you can adapt. Like your adjustment to maternity leave, the unfamiliar becomes familiar. Give it time. We know it seems impossibly trite, but trust us—it really will get easier.

Wherever you are on the spectrum, be sure to take one day at a time. If you're like us and are ready to quit before you even start, get through each day the best you can without worrying about how to change everything now. One coping strategy is to set a "reevaluate" date. Pick a date two to three months from when you return to work. Mark it on your calendar, and tell yourself that until that date you're going to muddle through. Then, when the date arrives, you'll be able to reassess your career and mothering plans with a much clearer head and more experience.

 reevaluate date

Don't race for the exit door yet. The emotions you feel in the first few weeks are raw and can lead you to believe that working motherhood is miserable or impossible. It's not! Give yourself a couple months before making any big decisions—about your job, breastfeeding, or moving to the sticks and living the "simple life."

BOSOM BUDDIES

For us, the saving grace was forming a support group of other working, nursing moms, and writing about our experiences in a journal. Being able to share our questions, fears, hopes, joys, and frustrations got us through the first few weeks and sustained us longer than we could have imagined.

You, too, must surround yourself with other working, nursing moms. During your ups you'll motivate each other; during your downs you'll find the support you need. If there's a lactation room where you work, start a journal as we did. If not, join our online journal at milkmemos.com. Stay in touch with moms you met in prenatal yoga or swimming, hospital birthing class, or Mommy and Me. Contact anyone you know who is a new working mom. Find new mommy friends by "flirting" with other moms at the pediatrician's office, at church, in the library, or at your neighborhood park. Any woman carrying a breastpump bag is a sure target. Once you're tuned in, you'll be surprised how many moms you see carrying pumps.

Your journey as a new working, nursing mom will be easier and less lonely with the support of other moms who can relate to boobs in breastshields. In our experience at IBM, we all had doubts and questions. There were days we felt like giving up. Quitting work or quitting nursing or locking ourselves in the lactation room and crying. There were good days too! It was fun to share all the baby pictures and funny stories, and to brag about first teeth, first solid foods, and first words with friends who were genuinely interested. These high points carried us through the blues and kept us pumping. Find friends. This is your assignment, it's mandatory, and there will be a test.

ON YOUR MARK, GET SET, PUMP!

As you prepare for that first week back, besides bracing yourself emotionally, you'll need to prepare lactationally, so to speak.

Thursday, March 15

Tragedy! I had to THROW AWAY three bags of frozen milk last night! I worked so hard to stockpile milk before coming back to work. I filled the bags to the top mark, and they burst in my freezer. Duh—the milk expanded when it froze. Now my freezer has icy breastmilk flakes all over it. I'm barely coping as it is, and now this has to happen.

Cate

P.S. How much frozen milk did you have stockpiled when you returned to work?

Thursday, March 15

Cate,

That is the WORST! Why do those breastmilk freezer bags even have a mark that high? One tip that someone told me is to freeze milk in small portions (one to three ounces). This prevents your nightmare explosion, and also makes it easy to thaw only a small amount when you need to top off a bottle.

Every mom has experienced her share of milk tragedies. My latest is that my day-care provider gave *my* breastmilk to another baby by accident. And George got some stranger's milk. How weird is that??

Stacy

P.S. You don't want to know how much frozen milk I had stored up. I'm a milk machine. I had about 120 ounces. But don't worry—you'll be OK if you have at least a couple bottles' worth. You'll add to it as you go along.

Thursday, March 15

That milk story gives me the heebie-jeebies! But if you think about it, the upper classes were raised on wet nurses' breastmilk for centuries, and no one seemed to find it odd or creepy. And we drink milk all the time from some strange *cow*! Still . . . it does freak me out to think of Charlotte drinking someone else's milk. It's such an intimate thing.

Thanks for the tip. Post–milk tragedy, I have 22¼ ounces, but who's counting?

Cate

You've probably lain awake at night wondering how much milk you should have stockpiled in frozen reserves before going back to work. Our answer? As much as you can. It's always nice to have extra milk when your baby needs it. One Milk Mama cleared the entire top shelf of her freezer to make room for her "milksicles." Others squeezed them in right next to the ice cream and Lean Cuisines. One over-achieving Milk Mama had pumped five hundred ounces before returning to work and had to purchase a second freezer for her garage. (We hate her.)

At a minimum, you need to pump as much milk as your baby will drink while you're at work that first day. Of course, that's the problem: when we nurse our babies we have no idea how much they're drinking. It would be so much simpler if God made babies with a little empty/full gauge! Why can't our breasts be like gas pumps with numbers flashing past to tell us how much is going in the tank? "Just one more quick squeeze to top it off to an even four ounces." An exclusively breastfed baby between one and six months of age typically needs nineteen to thirty ounces in a twenty-four-hour period, which means about eight to eleven ounces during a nine-hour workday. So you will need to have eight to eleven ounces of fresh milk for your baby to drink on your first day back. We recommend that you have a backup supply of at least three workdays' worth (twenty-four to thirty-three ounces) in the freezer. You'll replenish the fresh supply with what you pump each day at work, and you'll use the frozen supply for those times when your fresh supply runs short.

how much breastmilk to stockpile

1. *Estimate your baby's milk consumption/needs in a workday.* If you have done some trial runs expressing breastmilk and bottle-feeding your baby, you might have an idea of how much he typically drinks. If not, bear in mind the average in-

takes discussed above. You probably have an idea of whether your baby is at the higher or lower end of the range. See page 102 for more information on how much milk babies typically need.

2. *Provide at least one workday's worth of milk for your baby on your first day back*. Be as generous as you can with your pumped milk. Ask your child-care provider to document your baby's intake at each feeding (see page 353 for a sample log), and communicate clearly if you would like any unused milk to be saved and reused. (See pages 119–21 for Breast-milk Storage, Thawing, and Warming Guidelines.)

3. *Store as much backup supply as possible in your freezer*. If possible, reserve at least three workdays' worth of breastmilk in your freezer.

If you're worried about pumping milk for your stockpile while also giving your baby enough to drink, plan ahead. One Milk Mama said that, looking back, she wished she had started pumping during the first several weeks postpartum when her breasts were eager to fulfill their new milk-making role and she woke up with cantaloupes on her chest every morning. In general, you produce the most milk in the morning, so during your maternity leave, pump a few ounces either before your morning nursing or right after.

Some Milk Mamas find it easier to pump just before going to sleep, after their babies' last feeding. So if your baby nurses at 8:00 P.M., you could pump at around 10:00 P.M. With any luck, your baby probably won't nurse again for several hours, giving you enough time to "refill."

WHAT TO BRING

Friday, March 16

You'd think I'd have pumping down to a science since this is my second time around, but when I sat down in here this morning, I realized that one of my little white membranes was missing. I had to skip pumping and drive home over lunch. How is it that a dime-sized flap thing could be the linchpin to this whole stupid pump?

Stacy

P.S. Congrats—you've almost made it through your first week!

Friday, March 16

That sounds like something I would do. Every time I set up my pump I'm afraid something will be missing. Do you

think we could convince the IBM sundry shop to carry spare
breastpump parts?

Cate

P.S. TGIF!!! I never thought this week would end.

And you thought packing a diaper bag was hard? Well, by
the time you've finished packing your pumping supplies,
you'll soon realize that for the next ten months, you'll be lugging the equivalent of a car battery to and from work each
day. The first thing you absolutely must bring to work with
you on that first day back is your pump and its many parts,
each of them critical! We know of more than one Milk Mama
who accidentally left a breastpump part at home, only to have
to turn back during rush hour traffic to get it. And whatever
you do, don't forget pictures of your baby! One Milk Mama
brought her baby's onesie to help her feel close to him. She
was convinced that the onesie not only helped her relax but
also boosted her production. Turns out she's right; when you
conjure up an image of your baby through sight, smell, or
sound, your brain releases oxytocin, the hormone that helps
you relax and stimulates milk letdown.

🍼 pump-at-work essentials

Use this checklist to make sure you're ready to pump on your first day back.

- [ ] Breastpump with all the parts. Pumps vary, but generally include the following parts:
    - [ ] 2 breastshields
    - [ ] 2 pieces of tubing
    - [ ] 2 sets of valves that attach to the breastshields to enable suction (don't forget the small membranes)
    - [ ] 4 pump-attachable milk collection bottles
    - [ ] Ice packs (if pump includes milk cooler/storage compartment)
    - [ ] Just-in-case extras: 2 additional milk-collection bottles and lids; a few milk-storage bags with Ziploc closures
- [ ] 1 roll of paper towels and/or a couple burp cloths to wipe up spills (eek!) and dry your breasts after pumping
- [ ] Something to clean your pump parts (one or more of the following):
    - [ ] Small container of liquid dish soap plus drying rack (space permitting)
    - [ ] Antibacterial wipes
    - [ ] Microwave sterilizer bags

- [ ] Pictures of your baby!
- [ ] Journal and pen
- [ ] If needed, depending your pumping situation:
  - [ ] Extension cord or power strip
  - [ ] Car power adapter
  - [ ] If you don't have access to a refrigerator, and your pump doesn't include a milk cooler/storage compartment, bring a small insulated cooler plus ice packs
  - [ ] If you'll be storing your breastmilk in a community refrigerator, bring a small reusable lunch bag to keep your milk bottles/bags private and secure

MAMMARY MISSION

On your first day back, Milk Mama, you're going to have a mission: find a place to lactate! At IBM, we were fortunate to have a lactation room, even though it left much to be desired. We're not sure what we expected, but was it too much to ask for a clean chair with two armrests?

Monday, March 19

Did you ever stop and think, what kind of a name is "Lactation Room"!? Do we call the restroom a *Urination* room??? People view breastfeeding as another bodily function, but actually, we're preparing a meal for our babies. I certainly don't cook dinner in my bathroom at home!

Stacy

Monday, March 19

Good point on the name! But this room does have redeeming qualities. This lovely, brown medical table *is* padded and just comfortable enough for me to curl up and take a quick nap (ha!). Must remember pillow and blanket tomorrow . . .

Cate

Monday, March 19

Love the nap idea! While we're on the subject of our fancy lactation room, allow me to highlight some of its extra features.

1. A bulletin board with two pins.
2. Funky '80s art, from IBM Family Day at Watson Park. (Someone must have seen the word "family" and figured it belonged in this room.)
3. Medical table with file drawers full of old paper gowns.
4. Colorectal cancer brochures—plenty to go around, although they were printed in 1989.

Tuesday, March 20

Stacy,

Thanks for pointing out the amenities. Here are a few more:

5. Beige cinder-block walls
6. Dirty hospital flooring
7. Flickering fluorescent light

Cate

Tuesday, March 20

You forgot one: there's a mousetrap hiding in the corner behind the table!

Stacy

Unfortunately, most workplaces don't provide private lactation rooms, which makes for ever-increasing creativity and decreasing modesty for pumping moms. One Milk Mama who worked in a cubicle area pumped behind a decorative Japanese screen. She turned on a noise maker to drown out the droning breastpump *errrrruh errrrruh errrrruh* sound. Another who shared her office with a man boldly pumped milk right there next to him! He eventually took the hint and used that time to grab a cup of coffee or lunch. A more modest Mama pumped alone in her office, but because her door had no lock, she posted a picture of a dairy cow on the door with a sign that read PLEASE KNOCK. One Mama's office lock worked only from the outside of the door—she had to ask her coworker to lock her in and then let her out again. Another worked in a Manhattan office building that used to house a furrier. She pumped in the old fur vault, feeling a little too secure behind the fifty-pound steel door. If your company doesn't have a lactation room (or vault) and none of the other options sounds appealing, you can also pump in your car with your favorite music playing (and with a sun shade or towels covering the windows). Or you could try an empty conference room or the ladies' restroom. Please don't pump in a stall! We know, a stall is the only private spot in a restroom, but for starters, there's usually not even a toilet seat lid to sit on. Who wants to sit wearing business slacks on an open toilet, pumping milk for her newborn child? No woman should be reduced to this. Instead, roll an office chair into the bathroom and pump out in the open, facing the corner, and casually chat with women as they walk in. Other moms will understand, and if someone balks, use it as an opportunity to begin making your case for a private lactation room.

WHEN TO PUMP

Have you ever noticed that there's no good time to buy gas? The same goes for finding time to pump breastmilk during a busy workday. It's simply *not* convenient. There's always a meeting that runs long, a customer needing attention, or a million other demands. Starting day one, commit to setting aside two twenty-minute pumping sessions per day (midmorning and midafternoon, ideally when your baby would normally nurse). Think of yourself as a lioness providing for and protecting your cub. God help anyone who gets in your way!

Thursday, March 22

It's 5:45 P.M. I got assigned a "special project" this afternoon—just what I need, especially on Charlotte's 4 month birthday! The project required a 4:30–5:30 meeting so: (1) I'm missing 30+ minutes of my precious evening time with Charlotte, and (2) I'm pumping at 5:45 to try to keep up with what Charlotte will need tomorrow, when I should be home nursing her! Now I won't have enough for her when I get home. ARGH!

Cate

Friday, March 23

New top-secret special project consumed me from 10:30–2:30 today and I'm just now pumping! I'm so frustrated I could scream! I'm working on the project with a middle-aged male VP. I kept saying casually, "There's something I need to do by 1:00 for about 15 minutes. Would now be a good time to step away?" And he would say, "No, I think we're almost done. Let's just wrap this up." And there I sat feeling my breasts getting fuller and heavier, and I was thinking of little Charlotte and then my milk would let down and I would press my forearms against my breasts hoping they wouldn't leak.

Cate

Monday, March 26

Cate,

Next time just say, "Please excuse me. I've gotta go pump some *breastmilk* for Charlotte because I am a *mommy* and a *mammal* and my daughter needs my milk! So there!" Show me a male VP who will argue with that!

Stacy

P.S. I am woman, hear me MOO!

Monday, March 26

My week is not getting off to a good start! I made the mistake of wearing a dress (one of the few items in my "professional" wardrobe that fits my motherly body). Clearly, this wasn't my brightest moment. Now I'm here with my dress hitched up to my armpits revealing my granny panties (not back in bikinis yet!) and I'm FREEZING!

Cate

Monday, March 26

Cate,

I did the same thing my first week back with Colby. That's one of those mistakes that you only make once.

Hang in there, Stacy

PUMPING LIKE A PRO

Before long, you'll be proud of your pumping prowess!

Tuesday, March 27

Hey—I've learned a new trick for pumping and writing at the same time. Right now I'm holding both suction cups with my right hand while writing with my left. Proof point: women (especially moms) are superior multitaskers!

Cate

Tuesday, March 27

Cate,

See—you *are* making progress. Next thing you know you'll be pumping, writing, chewing gum, listening to a conference call, and scrambling eggs! My technique is to sit close to the table with the bottles wedged between the table and my breasts so that I have both hands free! Another method is to balance one bottle on your leg so you can write with that hand—this is much easier the second time around because your boobs are so saggy they just naturally rest on your legs! A good friend of mine actually rigged up a hands-free suction-cup-holding contraption out of a coat hanger and duct tape! I told her to enter it into her older son's science fair! I later learned that Medela actually sells a hands-free kit. Too bad my friend didn't patent her invention!

Stacy

Tuesday, March 27

Oh dear—I thought the sagginess was temporary. Am I doomed for life? Well, my breasts will have served their true purpose. They deserve to relax and be saggy.

Cate

P.S. Charlotte is a little roly-poly—she rolls over from her tummy to her back all the time now (so much for tummy time).

OVER THE HUMP

Once you get through the first week, you can breathe a sigh of relief. You survived. Your baby survived. Eventually, you'll start to believe that it just might be possible to blend motherhood, nursing, and career. We did it, lots of Milk Mamas have done it, and you can too!

TWO

* * *

pump and circumstance

Monday, April 2

Hi, my name is Andrea. Today is my first day back, and thanks to Cate I'm joining your little pumping club. My son's name is Caleb and he's 2½ months old. I also have two older kids—Cody 10, and Sierra 7, so I thought I was already prepared to juggle work and motherhood. But instead I feel completely lost and clueless about milk supply, milk pumping, milk mixing, milk storing . . . milk everything. My older kids are from my husband's first marriage (they live with us 50% of the time), so I've never had a newborn or nursed before. When I met Sierra, she was already potty trained and could put on her shoes. I didn't realize how much work it takes to reach that point! I feel like Caleb is helpless and needs me, but here I am at work. It helps to know he's with my aunt or mom while I'm here, but I still miss him like crazy.

Andrea

P.S. I see that you two have the same sleek leather pumping bag. What gives? My pump seems to do the trick, but it certainly didn't come with such a fancy black carrying case.

Monday, April 2

Welcome, Andrea! The more moms the merrier, even though you don't feel merry now! You're not alone. If you ever come down here and the door is locked, just knock and we can have a pumping party. I'm in here at around 10:00 and 2:00 every day—and will be for the next 9 months. My little George is almost 3 months too. What's Caleb's b-day? George's is Jan. 10.

Stacy

Monday, April 2

Andrea,

I'm glad you made it down here! Where is your pump? You can just leave it in here during the day. Stacy and I have the Medela Pump In Style. I'm sure they're all similar, so don't worry if it doesn't look the same. And you can direct all of your milk questions to Stacy, our resident milk expert. She nursed and pumped for her older son, Colby, for a whole year. She's my role model Mama! I'm going for a year with Charlotte.

Stick with us sister, Cate

Monday, April 2

Cate,

I didn't leave my pump in here because I was afraid you'd laugh at it. My motor is smaller than a coconut and the hoses are about as thick as coffee stirrers. I don't want it to feel like a Ford Fiesta parking next to a Lexus sedan.

How much do you guys pump in a session? I'm getting hardly anything. I can't even imagine pumping with this thing for a year. At the rate I'm going, I'll be lucky if I can pump until Caleb is 4 months old. By the way, Caleb and George were born 5 days apart (Caleb's b-day is Jan. 15)!

Clueless, Andrea

Monday, April 2

Andrea,

How fun that George and Caleb are so close in age! We can compare notes and race to see who rolls over first (the babies, I mean). Just kidding. I hate it when moms try to one-up each other on their babies' accomplishments—like it means they're superior! As for the pump, I've never tried anything other than my Pump In Style, but I can tell you that this thing sucked milk from me for a year with no problem, and it's still going strong for George. I like it because it's fast, not too heavy, and doesn't mind being dropped every once in a while. The built-in cooler keeps the milk cold all day (I sometimes put my yogurt smoothies in there too!). Don't worry, though; you can leave your little Ford Fiesta in here. We won't laugh. Well, maybe a little chuckle every now and then . . .

Stacy

Tuesday, April 3

Andrea,

Besides what Stacy said, the PIS (obviously not meant to be used as an acronym) is conveniently disguised as a briefcase for us working gals. Of course, it's twice as thick and heavy as a briefcase—and I would prefer a more "hip" design (pink polka dots?). But the other day, someone stopped me in the hall and asked me where I found such a nice leather bag! I thought about opening it to show her what was really inside, but then decided to let her think I was just incredibly fashionable instead.

Cate

Tuesday, April 3

Hey—how about a PIS "briefcase" with a funky cow print on it?

Stacy

Tuesday, April 3

Yes! I would totally buy one and would pay $20 extra! Why hasn't Medela thought of that already?

Cate

Tuesday, April 3

Well, it looks like I missed the memo about the PIS. I bought my pump because the packaging said, "For occasional separation of mother and baby." Since I work from home Thursdays and Fridays, I figured three days of pumping at IBM counted as "occasional separation." Wishful thinking on my part, I know. Now I'm wishing I had splurged for the real thing. My pump takes forever, and the motor is already making loud whining and clicking sounds. This thing should have come with earplugs. The people in the conference room next door are probably wondering why it sounds like someone is using a chainsaw in the Lactation Room.

Pumping Out Of Style (POOS),

Andrea

P.S. The automatic sinks in the bathroom are driving me nuts. Has anyone figured out how to stand at the perfect angle so the faucet will stay on for longer than two seconds while rinsing breastshields?

Wednesday, April 4

Andrea,

Try using the sink farthest to the left. For some reason, it stays on longer than the others (6 seconds instead of 2).

Stacy

BREASTPUMPS 101

Shopping for a breastpump can feel like the first time you set foot into a Babies "R" Us store and tried to pick items for your gift registry. It's overwhelming. There are manual/hand pumps, battery or electric pumps, portable electric pumps, one- or two-sided pumps, piston pumps (yikes!) and hospital-grade pumps. But as a working mom, your choice is really pretty simple. If you plan to use your pump more than once per day, you need a professional grade, portable, simultaneous double electric pump that cycles fifty–sixty times per minute. Don't settle for less.

It's important to start off with the right breastpump because the better your pump is able to mimic your baby nursing, the better it will stimulate your letdown and milk production, thereby helping you maintain your supply. When your baby nurses, she sucks about once every second. Don't buy a pump with a low cycling rate, or a pump that only "milks" one breast at a time, because they're slower than your baby, and much less efficient. You can also rule out a manual pump, which not only takes forever but will give you hand cramps after about three minutes. Suction strength is also important. Breastpump suction can range from 20 to 650 mmHg ("millimeters of mercury," a unit of pressure). Don't worry about the science of it all. Just know that pressures in the 250 range can be painful (we don't even want to think about what 650 would feel like!), while pressures below 150 are comfortable but ineffective. Look for a pump with a pressure between 200 and 230. Also, keep in mind that a pump with alternating double suction is less effective than a pump with simultaneous double suction. Simultaneous pumps cut pumping time in half versus single pumping—a benefit that will come in handy when you only have a few minutes to pump before helping a customer or getting to your next meeting. The smaller the pump, the louder the motor. Since you'll probably be pumping in an office, a bathroom, or somewhere else where privacy is lacking, you'll want a pump that doesn't attract attention.

breastpump requirements and recommendations

Make sure your pump meets the following standards:

- Electric (not a manual hand pump)
- Professional or hospital grade
- Convenient to carry (backpack, shoulder strap, or fits easily in a tote bag)
- Simultaneous, adjustable double suction
- Suction pressure in the range of 200 to 230 mmHg
- Cycle rate of 50 to 60 times per minute

Pumps that meet these requirements include:

- Medela retail: Pump In Style, Pump In Style Advanced, Pump In Style Limited Edition
- Medela hospital grade: Symphony, Lactina Select
- Ameda retail: Purely Yours
- Ameda hospital grade: Elite

BREAK OPEN THE PIGGY BANK

Thursday, April 5

I think HR has visited our janitor closet. Check the memo on the bulletin board.

Stacy

Thursday, April 5

What?! I can't believe IBM offers a 50% rebate on breast-pumps! The memo is dated January, so why are they just now pinning this up in April?! Besides, by the time someone in this room sees the memo, they have already paid *full price* for a pump and are in here *using* it. I wonder if I can get a rebate now, 5 months after buying my pump. I could use the $125 refund toward a high chair!

Cate

The only drawback to purchasing a professional-grade pump is the price. A good pump will set you back approximately $150 to $300. This sounds like a lot, but if you're planning to pump for more than six months or may have other little mouths to feed in the future, it's worth it. The right pump will get your milk supply off to a good start, and enable you to keep pumping and nursing as long as you wish.

Rationalize the cost of purchasing a pump by thinking of it as a priceless investment in your baby's health. You wouldn't buy a cheap car seat that may or may not hold up, so don't skimp on the purchase of a breastpump either. Besides, because you are feeding your baby breastmilk, you're spending less (or no) money on formula, which is a huge savings in itself.

If you're not sure that pumping will work for you or if you only plan to pump for a few months, consider renting a pump from a local hospital for approximately $40 to $70 per month (depending on where you live and what type you rent), plus an initial cost of about $40 to $50 for parts. Most hospitals rent the Medela Lactina piston pump (not as scary as it sounds!). Don't worry about the size of the clunky blue plastic carrying case—the pump itself is about the size of a shoe box. You can ditch the case and carry the pump along with your parts in an inconspicuous tote bag.

🍼 save on breastpumps

Before investing in a breastpump, check with your employer to see if they offer a discount or rebate.

Some insurance companies will partially or fully reimburse you for the purchase or rental cost of a breastpump. This depends upon how your insurance company covers medical equipment. Some insurers require a doctor's prescription.

CLEANING CALAMITIES

Monday, April 9

Stacy,

Thanks for the tip about the left sink. I was getting so frustrated that I considered heading to the drinking fountain to wash my pump parts (desperate moms must take desperate measures!). I read somewhere that it's very important to wash your pump after using it, but these sinks are ridiculously inconvenient. How anal are you guys about cleaning your parts (OK, that came out wrong, but you know what I mean)?

Andrea

Monday, April 9

Andrea,

I do the best I can with Palmolive and the cool water from the bathroom sink, but I am religious about sterilizing the parts when I go home. I throw everything into the top rack of the dishwasher and make sure I run it every night. Once I made the mistake of putting my parts into the dishwasher on a night we had spaghetti for dinner. The red from the spaghetti sauce stained all the plastic, which explains why my suction cups have sort of an orangeish tinge to them!

Cate

Tuesday, April 10

Disaster! Last night I decided to throw my pump parts into a pot of boiling water to sterilize them. I know you're only supposed to boil everything for 10-20 minutes, but I completely forgot the pot was on the stove and decided to go grocery shopping while Roger and Caleb had "boys' night out." When I came home an hour later, I opened the door and smelled "something" burning! Needless to say, the water had completely boiled off, and all that was left in the pot was an amorphous lump of smoldering plastic! Oh, I feel like such an idiot! Surely no other mom has ever been THIS dumb. My husband said I should be happy the house didn't burn down.

Now I'm here at work but have to leave twice to nurse Caleb (a blessing in disguise), because I am officially sans pump—and not looking forward to forking out the cash for another one. Thought I'd stop in here to share my misery with you guys. I'm not sure I can survive this whole pumping and working thing.

Juggling too many things at once, A

Tuesday, April 10

Andrea,

That is totally something that would happen to me! Hang in there, sister. Look at the bright side. You can now be in our PIS club *and* take advantage of the 50% rebate!

Cate

Tuesday, April 10

True confession: I almost never sterilize my pump parts. I was a sterilizing queen when I had Colby, but George gets the germs—and so far, he's alive and well. I relaxed my standards big-time the day I went to nurse George and had to first remove two dog hairs from my breast. How sanitary is that? I think scrubbing parts with soap and water after each use is sufficient (the pump parts, I mean!).

Stacy

The official rule for pump cleaning is that you should wash with hot, soapy water after each use, and sterilize daily. Unless milk gets into the tubes, you don't need to run water through them. If you see milk in the tubing, rinse with hot water and hang them to air dry. To dry them more quickly, or if condensation forms in the tubing, run your pump with only the tubes attached for a few minutes.

As with everything else, each mom has her own standard when it comes to cleanliness. You don't have to boil your pump parts or bottles in a pot of water. You can sterilize them in the dishwasher (only if you use the high-temperature wash and dry setting) or use microwave sterilizer bags or a microwave steam sterilizer. Yes, the same microwave you love for cooking bacon, popcorn, and baked potatoes you will now love for sterilizing plastic—in about four minutes flat! Another option for keeping your parts clean while at work is antibacterial wipes. You can buy specialty breast-pump wipes from Medela, but really any brand will do.

SHARE AND SHARE ALIKE?

Manufacturers recommend that you don't use a previously owned pump, yet they encourage renting a pump if you don't want to purchase one. So what's the difference? According to Medela, their rental pumps (such as the Symphony, Classic, and Lactina) are designed to be used by multiple women because they have barriers and filters that prevent milk from entering the pump motor. Personal pumps (such as the Pump In Style) don't have these special barriers/filters. Instead, they have an internal diaphragm that can't be removed, replaced, or sterilized. The concern is that bacteria and viruses may be transmittable through breastmilk or air, which could possibly enter the motor via the tubing. So there's a chance your baby could get sick if you borrow a pump, even if you use new breastshields and tubing.

Of course, the above advice is coming from a business whose profit depends on selling new breastpumps, so take it with a grain of salt. We've never met a Mama whose milk backwashed all the way through the tubing. We do know many moms who shared pumps but purchased their own tubing, bottles, breastshields, and other doodads. Maternity stores, hospitals, and even pump manufacturers sell the parts individually. If you go this route, be aware that personal

pump motors are not as robust as those in hospital-grade
rental pumps. Medela guarantees their personal pump motors for a year, but if you borrow a pump, you have no way
of knowing if it's operating with its original speed of suction—and there's no telling when it might run out of steam.
An inefficient motor draws less milk from you, and therefore
can compromise your milk supply. Use common sense; it's
best not to borrow a pump from your girlfriend who has
three kids and pumped for three years, but it's probably OK
to borrow a pump that's only been used for a couple of
months.

Wednesday, April 11

Wow! Pumping Nirvana. I am the proud owner of a
Pump In Style. This thing rocks! I'm producing almost twice
as much in about half the time. Maybe Caleb won't starve
after all! I'm so happy I could do an infomercial! That's a
funny thought—can you imagine a breastpump infomercial? A bunch of women sitting around pumping while en-
thusiastically praising their marvelous breastpumps. "I just
pumped 7 ounces of delicious, nutritious breastmilk in ONLY
10 MINUTES!" Call now and receive this miracle nipple

ointment ABSOLUTELY FREE. That's right! You will have the breasts of a 19-year-old. See Andrea before and after! (Dramatization. Results not typical.)

Pumped Up! A

Wednesday, April 11

A,

Congratulations on your luxury breastpump purchase. Now that you're in The Club, next time I see you I'll teach you the secret handshake (hint: you squeeze the other person's hand as if you're milking a cow).

Cate

Wednesday, April 11

Maybe a breastpump infomercial is exactly what we need to convince more new working moms to use this room and continue breastfeeding. I'll call Medela and offer to let them come film a pumping party right here in our closet.

Stacy

OUCH!

Wednesday, April 11

Me again with another question. Is pumping ever painful for you? I wonder if I'm getting sore from pumping too long. Do you think pumping for three hours straight is overdoing it? Just kidding! Seriously, with my old clunker I pumped for 30+ minutes when possible (don't tell my manager). Now I pump for about 20 minutes. I'm trying to squeeze every little drop out because my supply is so low. Or maybe I'm in pain because of this new high-powered pump. My little breasts don't know what hit them.

Andrea

Thursday, April 12

Andrea,

You reminded me of the first time I tried pumping. About 6 weeks before I returned to work with Colby, I bought my new "friend" but was afraid to go near her. She just sat there on the bathroom counter for a week. Finally I mustered up the courage to hook myself up. With sweaty palms I turned her on and . . . nothing! No milk. My nipples were stretching out to 6 inches long (I wasn't prepared for that sight!)

but nothing was coming out. My husband offered to "help." Being a guy, he naturally cranked the speed and suction dials up to the *max*. Holy COW!! I thought my breasts would fly across the room!

Other than that unforgettable incident, pumping has never been painful for me, and I don't think it ever should be. I think you should experiment with turning the dials down and/or limiting your pumping to 10 minutes for a while.

Stacy

If pumping is uncomfortable for you, something is wrong. Of course, stuffing your sensitive breasts into plastic suction cups for ten to fifteen minutes of tugging and sucking several times a day will never be as pleasant as getting a back rub, but it shouldn't hurt. To avoid pain while pumping:

- *Use the right pump.* A high-quality, efficient pump will provide the maximum comfort while producing the most milk. See page 50 for more on finding the right breastpump.
- *Use the pump correctly.* Make sure the suction speed or settings aren't turned too high. Center your nipple in the breastshield. Don't pump too long (fifteen minutes per session should be plenty).

- *Accommodate your breast size.* If you have small nipples or breasts and have been using the plastic insert in your breastshield, try removing the insert to see if that makes pumping more comfortable (or vice versa).

    If you have large nipples or breasts, make sure your breastshield is large enough. You can contact your pump manufacturer to super-size your shields. Medela makes a Personal Fit shield and even Dolly Parton–size glass shields (no, we're not kidding).

- *Watch for thrush.* While it may not be visible on your breasts, the fungal infection thrush creates a milky-looking residue on your baby's tongue. Thrush can make swallowing painful for your baby and nursing or pumping painful for you. (For more on thrush, see pages 181–82.)

Monday, April 16

Stacy,

Thanks for your sage advice. I'm going to try pumping for only 10 minutes, but I think I better add a third pumping session to eke out as much milk as possible. Too bad I don't get Frequent Pumper Miles. I could use a vacation already!

Andrea

THREE

. . .

blend until smooth

Monday, April 16

Caleb's latest talent is smiling at me. There is nothing cuter. I could spend forever just smiling back at him. Isn't it amazing to watch them learn each little thing? I hate missing even a minute of it. It's just not the same hearing about Caleb's day from my aunt or mom.

Andrea

Monday, April 16

Andrea,

I know what you mean about missing the smiles. Charlotte's new skill is putting her toes in her mouth. She's a little pretzel! Mondays are the worst. Right now my stomach feels like a washing machine on spin cycle. Or a dryer, with tennis shoes in it. After the first couple weeks back at work I didn't think it could get any worse, but I was wrong. Instead of enjoying and savoring every moment I had with Charlotte this weekend, I found myself dreading coming to work. It's bad enough to have to leave Charlotte every day, but now IBM is creeping in on what little time I have with her at home. I can't stand being here with this mechanical pump while my nanny or Chris holds Charlotte and feeds her breastmilk from a plastic bottle. Totally depressing. I'm not at all sure I can pull this working mom thing off.

Sorry to be such a downer!

Cate

Monday, April 16

I am right there with you, and on top of being brokenhearted, I am feeling totally overwhelmed at work. It's sort of like trying to join a sprinting race 10 seconds after the starting gun has sounded. I feel like I'm in last place and there's no way to catch up because the other runners are all toned and fit, and I've been out of the race for 3 months. It's not that I've been sitting on the couch eating bonbons; I've just been playing another sport called motherhood! Need to get back in "running" shape. Frick.

Andrea

Monday, April 16

What's with all this heavy stuff? You guys need to take a deep breath and eat more chocolate. I know this is hard work, juggling career and motherhood. Take it a day at a time. You'll get into a groove, I know it.

I am sorry to say that I won't be here to keep you out of the dumps after tomorrow. We're leaving Wednesday morning for Kansas to visit my in-laws for a week. Wish me luck! They're nice people, but *very* proper and conservative. They're not so hip on me nursing. I think the whole thing just freaks them out. God forbid I should expose my breast at the dinner table, utter (ha!) the word "nipple," or nurse George in public. Sheesh, you'd think it was 1955.

Stacy

Monday, April 16

No! You can't desert us! You must have your cell phone on at all times in case we have a question. (Just kidding.) (Sort of.)

Cate

Tuesday, April 17

Stacy,

We'll miss you! Have a safe trip. You'll have to tell us how the breast baring goes!

Andrea

Tuesday, April 17

Andrea and Cate,

I'll be thinking of you. Hang in there.

Your pumping pal,

Stacy

Some Milk Mamas start to feel better after the first few weeks, but don't beat yourself up if you're not one of them. Though you've gotten over the initial hump, the road ahead will have many ups and downs. The first week back at work is a bit of a reunion—your colleagues are excited to have you back, you're interested to hear about everything that's happened while you were in babyland, and your workload hasn't ramped up yet. After a few weeks, reality begins to set in. The things you loved about your work may not seem as appealing. The things you hated are still there. You haven't settled into a routine yet, you're sleep deprived, your brain is not functioning at 100 percent, you miss your baby like crazy, and you're preoccupied with wondering how he's doing in your absence.

Our advice? Don't give up! Recognize that you're in the midst of a huge adjustment. Gradually you *will* become more comfortable with the separation from your baby. This may not seem like much consolation, because who really wants to feel comfortable leaving her baby? But here you are. For whatever reason, you've already made the decision to return to work. Maybe you're the primary or only breadwinner, you love your job, staying at home full-time doesn't appeal to you, or you've become accustomed to the lifestyle that your income affords and want to see if you can make it work. The point is that every new mom who returns to work feels some degree of angst. Eventually we all need to believe that our babies will be fine in the care of another, but that no one will ever take our place as mommy in our children's hearts. Eventually it really is possible to adjust to being away from your baby. Be patient with yourself. Allow time to work its magic as you sort through the emotional and practical challenges of blending motherhood, breastfeeding, and career . . . until smooth.

Tuesday, April 17

For 13 years, I've been waking up each day and going to work at IBM. Why does it now feel so impossible? Does being a mother make you a totally different person? What has happened to the Cate who was confident, focused, driven, and ambitious? For some reason, I thought I would be able to return to work and still be the star employee while I'm here and the world's best mom at home. But instead, the mom in me is ever-present and the future executive in me seems to have flown the coop. When I was pregnant, I used to love the thought of two hearts beating inside my body, Charlotte's and mine. Even after giving birth to her, Charlotte's heart stays with me always—and I can't stop thinking about her.

Cate

Tuesday, April 17

We need more tissue in here. It's going to be a while before I can wear mascara to work again. It's hard to put into words how I feel, but I have a sadness and longing that consumes my heart. I look at Caleb in the mornings, smiling and kicking in his crib, and I want the whole world to stop. This morning, I tried to leave for work three times. I kept getting into my car and then going back in the house to see him one more time. I couldn't pull myself away. My husband, Roger, stayed home today with Caleb and Sierra, who has strep throat for the billionth time. Roger was watching me go back to see Caleb again and again . . . and he said, "Why are you torturing yourself?" All I could say was, "I don't know."

Because I have seen how quickly my older kids have

grown, I know how fleeting these moments are. I want to hold Caleb and never let go.

Sobbing, Andrea

Wednesday, April 18

This morning, I sat in my car for 5 minutes in the parking lot, trying to collect myself and stop crying. I thought an extra swipe of blush and lipstick would disguise my misery, but right as I walked in the door, I saw one of my best friends, who asked, "Are you OK?" Of course, then I started crying again. I don't want to be here. I want to be home. I feel totally disconnected from my job right now, yet I have to somehow go through the motions for another long week (and another and another . . .). On top of it all, I was up three times last night with Charlotte, so I'm a zombie. Stacy said this would get easier, but I think she's a big liar!

Cate

Wednesday, April 18

Cate,

I completely understand—we'll get through this together. Every day I say good-bye to Caleb and come to work, I try not to think about the fact that I'm helping pay maintenance to Roger's ex-wife—who, unlike me, got to be home with her kids when they were babies! I knew what I was getting into when I married Roger, but it's still a hard pill to swallow. Even though Roger makes good money working here at IBM, it's not enough to support two households—so I have to keep working. I can't wait until the day we're done with maintenance; that's the day I'll be asking to go part-time—and Roger and I will have a margarita party!

Andrea

Wednesday, April 18

What's maintenance? Alimony? What about you maintaining your sanity? Good Lord.

Cate

CAN YOU HAVE IT ALL?

It's the age-old question. Can you have a great, fulfilling career and still be the mom you want to be? Unfortunately, the answer is no—at least not during your first weeks and months back. Before having a baby, work was probably a major focus in your life and for the most part was conveniently separate from family life. Now you are faced with the challenge of blending devotion and love for your child with dedication and commitment to your career.

We have yet to meet a mom who dove back into her job with gusto, able to put thoughts of her baby aside until she returned home. Whether you love your job or hate it, whether you are eager to return to work or not, you're a mom now, and your very nature has changed.

Others may still expect you to be the same person as before. *You* may even try to be the same person. It's not possible. You've changed—for the better. Over time, you'll begin to define how much space your career needs and how much motherhood needs. The ratio is different for everyone, and you'll know when you're out of balance. During the first weeks and months, you'll probably feel out of balance a lot.

Thursday, April 19

I figured out one of the reasons I feel so conflicted. I've always proudly considered myself a feminist. I've wanted (and in fact I've earned) the opportunity to become an executive. But now I'm rethinking whether I'll actually pursue that opportunity . . . whether it's worth it to me. If I choose not to, does this automatically put me on the "mommy track"? Am

I letting other feminists down? I want a *woman* to be the CEO of IBM, the president of the United States, the leader of the free world. I just don't want that woman to be *me*. Surely other high-potential career moms feel differently?

Cate

Monday, April 23

Cate,

Someone once put it to me like this—men can advance their careers along a steady upward path. Women's lives tend to be more seasonal, and this is your season to be a *mom*. You can always get back on the career fast track later, when Charlotte is older (or not). For me, I've never really been on the fast track, partly because I "inherited" two young kids as soon as I started working here. I've had to balance family and work from day one. My manager and coworkers know that my family comes before my career, but that doesn't mean I have to stop being a valuable employee. Why should we feel guilty about loving motherhood? Immerse yourself in being a mom. Enjoy it. Celebrate it. And if that means you're labeled a "mommy" for this period in your life, accept the title as if someone had just told you you'd been named CEO.

Andrea

P.S. I just reread what I wrote. Sounds pretty convincing. Maybe someday I'll really believe it myself.

Monday, April 23

Andrea,

Thanks! Maybe the original feminists succeeded by giving us the freedom to choose our roles throughout our lives, and not let gender dictate who will pursue career and income and who will focus on parenting and nurturing. Of course, the luxury of choosing is not available to everyone. I struggle with what to do, yet I try to remember every day to count my blessings.

Cate

Now that we can have it all, do we want it? Would we actually rather choose the roles our mothers had, living in a time when women were expected to stay at home with the kids, and were judged by the fluffiness of their lemon meringue pies? Thank goodness we've moved beyond that, but with the "freedom" to work comes the challenge of harmonizing the roles of nurturer and breadwinner. Our goal, Milk Mamas, is to help shape a society in which women *and* men can openly and actively embrace parenthood without jeopardizing their careers or feeling guilty.

TWO WORLDS COLLIDE

Tuesday, April 24

Wow—I took a conference call while pumping this morning. How weird was that! I felt totally self-conscious as my nipples stretched out and back while I listened to people discuss long-range plans, key initiatives, critical dependencies, and milestones.

Cate

P.S. We tried feeding Charlotte rice cereal last night. I have mixed feelings about it. I know I can't always be her sole source of nutrition, but I'm not ready for her to go to the next stage. (I cried when she went from size 1 to size 2 diapers.) Chris is convinced the cereal will help her sleep through the night. She was pretty adorable opening her tiny mouth, sticking out her tongue, and grabbing the spoon.

Tuesday, April 24

I'm looking forward to Caleb's first solid food feast—I want him to fatten up. After all, this is the only time in life when pudgy rolls of fat are cute! That must have been bizarre to be on a conference call while pumping. I always wonder what everyone's doing during those calls. I've led calls before from home in my flannel PJs while eating peanut butter from a spoon. And I have a friend who claims to often take conference calls in the *nude*. Who knew?

Andrea

While at work, don't succumb to any suggestion (or temptation) to disguise your maternal self. One way to do this is to keep pumping! Some moms find comfort in pumping during the workday because it helps them feel connected to their babies and their motherhood. Others find pumping a hassle and a disruption. Either way, motherhood stares you in the face when you're at work, breasts exposed, pumping milk. It doesn't get more tangible than that. Let pumping while working be your stake in the ground that says, "I'm a mom, first and foremost." No apologies!

A MOTHER'S GUILT

Wednesday, April 25

Today I had to get here at 8 A.M. for a meeting. I was rushing around this morning with not nearly enough time to just *be* with Charlotte. Then I nursed her right before leaving and was trying to rush her—which, of course, is impossible. She had that half-asleep look of contentment, until I had to take her off my breast before she was finished nursing. She started groping for my breast but I had to lay her on the floor crying because I had to finish getting dressed and my nanny was running late. Now I can't get the image of Charlotte on the floor out of my mind! I want SO MUCH to be holding her!

C

Beware: guilt comes with the territory of being a working mom. If you're at work thinking about your baby, you may feel guilty that you're not totally focused on work. And, at some level, you may feel guilty for leaving your baby in the first place. If you have to take time off work to be with your baby for a doctor's appointment or if she's sick, you may feel guilty about that. Or you might find yourself loving your job and enjoying the time away, and then you may feel guilty for not feeling guilty. You can't win.

Stop the madness! Some degree of guilt is unavoidable, but don't let it creep in and take over like a nasty bindweed. You have a right to take your child to the doctor. Thinking and talking about your baby while at work is perfectly acceptable. Needing time away from your baby is OK too. Do the best you can and don't be too hard on yourself.

MILK MAMAS UNITE

Thursday, April 26

Nipple nipple nipple nipple nipple nipple nipple nipple. Breast breast breast breast breast breast breast breast. Ah—that feels better. I was totally cooped up at my conservative in-laws' house all last week. Day one of my vacation I was in their living room having a quiet nursing moment with George. Along came Barbara, who tossed an old brown afghan over us (mind you, they keep their thermostat at 75 degrees). George would have nothing to do with the blanket. He cried and yanked it down as fast as I could pull it up on my shoulder. And that was just day one!

I can see you two have been busy philosophizing in here! My thoughts later.

I was hoping George would learn to roll over while we were on vacation (so I could actually be there to witness a "first"). But he was far too fascinated by Grandma and Papa's ceiling fan to bother with rolling over. Plus, he just discovered how to open and shut his little hands, so that keeps him busy. Cute!

Stacy

P.S. Cate, how's the rice cereal/sleeping experiment going? Colby never liked rice cereal. If Charlotte rejects it, you might try pureed bananas, avocado, yams, or sweet potatoes, which are nutritionally better anyway. Also, you may have discovered that, unfortunately, there's no connection between starting cereal and getting more zzzzs. If only it could be that easy!

Thursday, April 26

Back again... here's my two cents on the working mom/career conflict. My mom stopped working when she got married and always regretted it. She's always encouraged me to continue working. Just because we work doesn't make us any less motherly. In fact, it probably makes me a better mom, because I'm more fulfilled. I think it works for us because I really like my job, and my manager is very flexible. I definitely make the most of that—to do kid drop-off *and* be home for dinner and bedtime every night. Also, because my husband, Bill, works at a small start-up, he works long hours but it doesn't have to be 8 to 5. I'm not saying it's easy. Whenever something happens at home or at work, like if Colby gets sick or a meeting keeps me at work late, things can get out of hand really quickly. It's probably this way for all families with two working parents—when one thing gets thrown off, the ripples are felt far and wide.

Stacy

Thursday, April 26

Welcome back, Stacy! You're right (of course) on the rice-sleep myth. We're going to give the cereal a rest for a few weeks.

What's Babs's address? I'm going to anonymously send a La Leche League brochure to their house. Along with a printout of the Kansas state law which protects a woman's right to breastfeed anywhere she has a right to be—like on the sofa in a house, for God's sake!

Cate

Monday, April 30

Forget the brochures. Let's organize a huge nurse-in on Barbara's front lawn!

A

home away from home

Stacy and Andrea,

I decided to bring a few items to make our clubhouse a little less "janitor closet" and a little more "pumping palace"! So far I brought some Clorox wipes and a few newer magazines. (I didn't throw away the May 1991 *Mainframe Monthly* magazine in case you're still reading one of the articles.)

Cate

Good idea, Cate! I'll pitch in by calling housekeeping to see if they'll clean this disgusting floor!

A

P.S. Thanks, I've already read that magazine cover to cover.

Tuesday, May 1

Ladies,

My contributions to the palace: soap and hand lotion for everyone to share, and I confiscated a paper towel roll which was left on the counter in the Building 2 bathroom! In our spare time (ha!) we should follow the housekeeping people as they make their bathroom cleaning rounds—I've noticed they sometimes throw out the paper towel rolls with towels *still on them*. Wow—just think—now we don't have to stand there waving at the paper towel motion sensor to get one six-inch towel at a time.

Fairy Godmother (Stacy)

Tuesday, May 1

Fairy Godmother,

Who knew we could get so excited about paper towels? I've already helped myself to our new community roll.

Andrea

Wednesday, May 2

Clean floor!

Stacy

Wednesday, May 2

Yea! ☺

A

Wednesday, May 2

Next improvement: Let's all bring in pictures of our babies and plaster them all over the walls! I'm going to see if I can get a life-size enlargement of Charlotte. I do work in the printing division, after all! Maybe they wouldn't mind printing a few hundred or so . . . just kidding! Let's start with this picture of Charlotte in her ExerSaucer! She loves grabbing the sparkly star and making the lights and music turn on. She's so delighted with herself—she can finally cause things to happen on purpose.

Cate

Wednesday, May 2

Charlotte's a genius!

Stacy

Wednesday, May 2

We put Caleb in his ExerSaucer a couple weeks ago but he is such a little peanut that the seat swallowed him up. We tried putting towels in the bottom to give him a boost, and he still could hardly see over the tray thing. Back to the bouncy seat, at least for now.

Andrea

CREATURE COMFORTS

No matter where you pump, it's important to create a space that makes you feel relaxed and comfortable. When you feel at ease, your milk will let down more readily and you may even produce more. Besides, you deserve a pleasant place to step away from your work and just be a mom.

If you are fortunate enough to have a lactation room, bring anything that makes the room feel homey—pictures of your baby, music player, magazines, a lamp with soft lighting, and a few logs for the fire (just kidding). If you're pumping in your office or a conference room, or you're a pumping "squatter," keep a few comfort items in your pumping bag— your favorite snack, pictures, and so on. For those of you who pump in your car, take an extra five minutes to drive to a more private spot away from your office parking lot. Move to the passenger seat (so the breastshields don't compete with the steering wheel). Slide the seat back, stretch your legs, and play your favorite song.

Monday, May 7

Who swiped the soap? It's missing. And I brought Caleb pics for the wall, but there's no tape! I don't think the two push-pins IBM generously provided on the bulletin board will penetrate the cinder-block walls.

A

P.S. Nobody would actually steal our soap, would they?

Monday, May 7

The pictures of Caleb are great. I brought some more of Charlotte. Don't they make a cute couple? Honestly, it's not too early to start thinking about prom!

Cate

Monday, May 7

When do you guys have time to print pictures??? My poor children's "photo albums" (using the term loosely) are probably going to go from hospital newborn photo to first-grade school picture. Sigh.

Stacy

Tuesday, May 8

I brought the tape and another essential item—chocolate kisses. Indulge! I also brought soap but am sorry to report that the bottle is completely empty because it leaked out all over my brand new Pump In Style. Frick!

A

Tuesday, May 8

Cripes! It's bad enough when your shampoo leaks in your cosmetic bag when you're traveling. Now you have a sudsy, sticky, lemon-scented pump!

Thanks for the chocolate. I hope you had a few pieces yourself after that incident.

Cate

Tuesday, May 8

This place is looking better by the day! Charlotte and Caleb are adorable. You won't believe what I did (being the Dorm Mother and all): I forgot my bottles. After a momentary panic I went to the cafeteria and helped myself to two coffee cups. The challenge was placing the coffee cups at just the right distance apart on the table, then holding my breastshields while hovering above the cups, and being careful not to knock one over. I'm exhausted. Need chocolate—thanks!

Of course, the PIS cooler doesn't exactly accommodate coffee cups, so now I have to put the cups in the Building 2 fridge and hope nobody disturbs them. Do you think I should mark them "STACY'S BREASTMILK. NOT HALF-&-HALF!"

Stacy

P.S. Little George rolled over!

Tuesday, May 8

How resourceful of you, Stacy! If that would have happened to me, I would have cried—all the way home to get my bottles.

Andrea

P.S. George wins. But can he say his ABC's yet? Caleb can! (kidding)

Tuesday, May 8

I brought in a few extra milk-storage bottles for emergency backup. I have extras because at the end of my maternity leave, my sister-in-law sent me a care package with milk storage bags, bottles, breastpads, lanolin, a water bottle, and a picture frame. How (bitter)sweet is that?

Also, since one of our outlets is flaky, I invested in a power strip for our clubhouse. Now we can have a real pumping party! BYOP.

Cate

Tuesday, May 8

Is there room for one more at your party? My name is Stephanie, and I have a little boy named Darren. He was born March 13, and I came back to work April 30. I wasn't able to take more than six weeks off because we live on my income. My husband, Chad, is a stay-at-home dad. He used to be an elementary-school teacher, and it made more sense financially for him to stay home vs. paying for full-time child care. It's been a tough adjustment for me. I know Chad is actually better suited to be a stay-at-home parent than I am, but I still feel jealous. I'm saving my two weeks of vacation so I can take time off over the next few months whenever I need to get a Darren fix.

Steph

P.S. What's with no guaranteed paid leave in this country? We should all move to Sweden, where parents get 18 months paid leave per child!

Wednesday, May 9

WELCOME STEPHANIE!

Don't get me started about paid leave. My friend in Canada got 35 weeks, and someone told me that moms in Bulgaria get two years! If that happened here, would we ever go back to work? What do you do, by the way? We'd love to see pics of Darren! My little one is Charlotte, and my husband, Chris, is a part-time stay-at-home dad. He went to a 2½-day-a-week schedule at IBM so he could be with Charlotte the other half of the week, at least through the first year.

Ladies, now that we have a cozy clubhouse, we should formalize our club. I even thought of a name: MILK— Mothers in Lactation Kinship!

Cate

Wednesday, May 9

That's perfect. Let's all meet here at 10:30 A.M. tomorrow (make sure no one follows you) and we'll make a secret MILK pact, which, naturally, we'll seal with drops of milk!

Hi, Stephanie!

Andrea (Caleb's mom)

P.S. What are you guys doing for Mother's Day? As a stepmom, it's always been a strange holiday for me. Of course, Cody and Sierra spend the day with their mom, and I usually spend the day feeling forgotten or invisible. Not this year! I want to wake up to breakfast in bed, a bouquet of flowers from the yard, and snuggles with Caleb. I wonder what it will be like when he actually can say the word "mom." What an honor. For now, I'll settle for his adorable smiles, coos, and babbles.

Wednesday, May 9

Thanks for the warm welcome. I'm a Product Engineer. I have to tell you upfront, I hate pumping, but maybe it will be easier in this palace! I've been pumping in my office, but now I have a new office mate—Dirk, the college intern, who takes his shoes off (STINKY FEET), and whose job seems to consist of e-mailing his friends, talking to his girlfriend on the phone, and eating BBQ potato chips all day. He works mornings, and goes to class in the afternoon. So I guess I'll be pumping in here every morning.

Steph

P.S. I'll bring pics.

Thursday, May 10

Stephanie,

Let's hope that Dirk doesn't discover BBQ pork rinds! A guy down the hall from me eats those. He cooks them at 10:00 every morning in the microwave (like popcorn), and they sizzle in the bag as they emit a totally disgusting smell. That's my cue to come here and pump!

Cate

Thursday, May 10

Welcome, Stephanie! I'm George's mom. Tell Dirk to get to work. And don't worry, we have a strict shoes-on policy here in our palace.

Stacy

P.S. Who is the THIEF? Was all set to pump and write, but the pen was missing. Tucked boob in, left shirt out, marched across the hall, and "borrowed" a pen from the credit union.

P.P.S. I'm all about breakfast in bed for Mother's Day!

CAN'T HURT TO ASK

No matter the size of your workplace, it's perfectly reasonable to expect support, space, and time for pumping. Few businesses proactively offer this because they don't realize the need exists and/or they are unaware of the benefits of lactation programs. Besides, let's face it, there are a lot of men running businesses who may enjoy thinking about breasts, but don't often think about breast*milk*. Let's change that.

To get the support, space, and time you need, you might have to educate your employer. Stand tall and state the facts.

lactation program benefits for employers

Providing a lactation program:

- *reduces absenteeism*—Breastfed babies are sick less often; therefore moms are absent less frequently from work. And when breastfed babies do get sick, they usually recover faster, so absences are shorter.
- *reduces health-care costs*—Companies save an average of $400 in health-care costs, per baby, over the first year.
- *improves employee job satisfaction and retention*—Lactation programs create a family-friendly atmosphere, resulting in higher job satisfaction and morale, greater company loyalty, and improved long-term employee retention. This also reduces the costs of recruiting, hiring, and training new employees.
- *enhances company image*—Companies that support breastfeeding enhance their ability to attract and retain new employees.
- *improves productivity*—When breastfeeding moms feel supported, they are more productive at work.

Source: Abbott Laboratories (interestingly, the company that makes Similac formula)

Start by asking for the basics: a clean, private room with a table, chair, electrical outlet, door, and no windows (or if there are windows, curtains are a must). Feeling bold? Ask for the room to be located near a bathroom or kitchen area where you can wash your bottles. Or try asking for the moon: a lactation room equipped with a hospital-grade pump for sharing. Instead of lugging a pump to work each day, each mom could bring her own personal set of breast-shields, tubing, bottles, and parts—and "hook up." (For more about hospital-grade pumps that are designed for multiple users see page 57.) The point is, don't be afraid to ask. You might be surprised by what you get in return.

DARE TO DREAM

Monday, May 14

Hope your Mother's Day was great. Chris surprised me with a corsage. I wore it to church and then out to brunch. My dad used to do that for my mom. I felt so proud and special. ☺

Cate

Monday, May 14

Had a dream-come-true Mother's Day. What did I do to deserve such happiness?

Still on cloud 9,

A

Monday, May 14

It's 75 degrees outside but I am freezing in here! I'm going to have to bring in my winter parka. Next on the clubhouse wish list: a space heater!

Steph

P.S. I'm the pen thief. Accident, sorry! It's back now. . . .

Monday, May 14

Brrrrrr . . . I agree! My milk is coming out already chilled. As long as we're making a wish list, how about:

1. Dorm-room-size refrigerator (or maybe not in a room this cold!)
2. ~~La-Z-Boy~~ (Not) La-Z-Mom recliners
3. Home theater with surround-sound (for movies and music)
4. Pull-out sofa for a little shut-eye
5. Best idea yet: pedicure while you pump!

Stacy

Tuesday, May 15

Yes! While we're reviewing applications for nail techni-
cians and waiting for our entertainment system to arrive,
here's another idea. Now that we've all brought pictures,
let's plan to create a Graduate Wall of Fame. When your
pumping days are over (can you imagine the day?), you get
to post a picture of your baby in a special place on the wall.
Include name (of baby and mom), date of birth, and date
you stopped pumping. The idea will be to honor each other
and to inspire other pumping moms. Think how great it will
be for a new mom to walk in here one day and see an entire
wall covered with pictures of smiling breastfed babies!
Won't that be awesome?

Cate

Tuesday, May 15

I love it! Can Colby be the first graduate? I know our
clubhouse didn't exist a few years ago, but I did manage to
pump/work/nurse for a full year. Besides, shouldn't he be
~~grandfathered~~ grandmothered in? While we're at it, can he
be class valedictorian?

Stacy

Tuesday, May 15

You guys are so gung-ho about breastfeeding. I wish I
shared your enthusiasm, but I don't. Darren was born at 32

weeks and weighed 3 pounds, 3 ounces, so we had a very rough start. He never figured out how to latch on, so I've been a full time pumper since he was born. At first I was making WAY more than he was drinking, so I have about 100 bags of frozen milk in my freezer, maybe more. So far, no formula, but I don't know how long I can keep it up. I would feel guilty for giving up pumping just because it's hard and inconvenient. I know how good it is for Darren, especially since he was a preemie.

Stephanie

Tuesday, May 15

Stephanie,

I can't believe Darren was a preemie . . . he is the cutest little pudge ball in the pictures!

To answer your question, Stacy, absolutely—on all counts!

Cate

Tuesday, May 15

Stephanie,

I give you so much credit for pumping even though you hate it, and you never got to enjoy nursing. That's dedication!

All,

I think we should also post pictures of ourselves next to our offspring, so we can see each other. Isn't it weird that we all pump in here but rarely at the same time? With pictures, we'll know who to give the secret MILK handshake to in the hallway.

P.S. I hope Caleb won't be the next graduate. My milk supply is pitiful, but now that I've achieved my goal of 4 months (yea me) there's no way I'm quitting now! Next goal: 6 months (July 15). Drip, drip . . .

Andrea

Even though lactation rooms don't (yet) come standard with La-Z-Boys, we *have* come a long way. Pumps have improved dramatically, and some employers are ever so slowly starting to accept (and a few even promote) breastfeeding. The generation before us, lacking electric pumps, had to squirt milk into Dixie cups in bathroom stalls. Our generation has double-shooter electric pumps and the example and support of other working, nursing moms. The hope for our daughters is that lactation rooms in the workplace will be as common as (but separate from!) restrooms. Milk Mamas, we must pave the way for moms who follow. We must help build the luxury lactation room of the future! Babies, moms, and businesses will all be better off.

FIVE

. . .

milk duds

Monday, May 21

Help! I have a weird problem: my right side only has a few sprinklers, takes forever, makes half as much milk as my left, and is about half the size. What's up with that?? I guess my supermodel career will have to wait until I'm done nursing. And while I'm on the subject, who knew that we had a bunch of tiny sprinklers in our nipples? I always imagined one hole in the center like a bottle. Crazy.

Cate

Monday, May 21

Cate,

You crack me up! Hey, I just thought of this:

Q: What do you call the side that doesn't produce much milk??

A: A "Milk Dud"——ha ha!

Well, I can't help but offer my advice. Maybe your right side produces less because you nursed Charlotte on that side last before coming to work? That happened to me with Colby—it took me a while to figure it out. Then I switched my routine and presto change-o, Milk Dud switcharoo! Or maybe I'm just freakishly symmetrical. Actually, it's common for one breast to produce more or less than the other.

Stacy the Milk Maestro

Tuesday, May 22

Stacy,

What would I do without your humor and advice? I think I'm the freak. My right side has always been the low producer, regardless of which side Charlotte nursed on last. In fact, I always nurse her on the right side first for that reason. Chris calls my left breast "Old Faithful"! Now I have a name for the right one, too: "Milk Dud"—I love it.

Lopsided,

Cate

Tuesday, May 22

Cate,

My right side is the same way! I barely produce any on that side. Actually, my milk production is low, period. It's amazing that Caleb has gained any weight, but at 4 months he's up to a whopping 12 pounds!

Andrea

Wednesday, May 23

Great news: CHARLOTTE SLEPT THROUGH THE NIGHT! Good news: Charlotte can sit up on her own now! What a big girl!

Bad news: I've started logging my milk production. Big mistake because now I'm obsessing. In the last three days, I pumped 2.75 to 3.5 ounces in the morning, and 2 to 3 ounces in the afternoon. That doesn't seem like enough! How much should I be making? How do I know what Charlotte needs?

Cate

Wednesday, May 23

I guess one good thing about pumping all the time is that I know how much Darren is getting! And as you pointed out Cate, he's quite the chubbo, with little rolls of fat even on his wrists. I love that!

Steph

HOW MUCH IS ENOUGH?

At one time or another, every Milk Mama on the planet worries about whether she is producing enough milk. When you're bottle feeding, you can actually see the milk disappear as it goes from the six-ounce line to the two-and-a-half ounce line. When you're breastfeeding, your breast gets a little smaller and squishier, but what does that tell you? Not much. Milk production is worrisome enough when we're home nursing our babies. But when we start pumping regularly at work and actually *see* how much (or how little) we're really making, this adds a new level of stress. While some moms (like us) painstakingly tap their plastic suction cups to get every last drop into the bottles, others (like Stacy) easily fill two bottles, and sometimes three!

Thursday, May 24

Cate,

Yea for Charlotte! My little George is so top-heavy with that giant head of his, I think he's going to topple over when he's old enough to sit.

To answer your question, I think milk supply (and how much our babies drink) is a very individual thing. I know my production is on the high side. For example, this morning I produced 13 ounces in one sitting (which is more than usual for me). I had to get a third bottle out! My doctor says that babies between 1 and 6 months need anywhere from 19 to 30 ounces a day. I'm sure George eats at least 30! After 6 months, he'll need less breastmilk because he'll start eating solid foods.

Stacy

Thursday, May 24

For what it's worth, I pump about 28 ounces a day. I get way more in the morning than in the evening. But I've never made as much as Stacy in a single sitting. I've always wondered if women with bigger breasts make more milk? I'm just an A cup Mama (B when nursing).

Steph

Thursday, May 24

Stacy,

OH MY GOSH, you are a Dairy Cow! I am so jealous I don't know if I can continue to be friends with you.

Well, OK. Just tell me your secret! Is it your buxom physique?

Cate

P.S. Do you mind if I call you Jugs?

how much milk your baby needs

- An exclusively breastfed baby's milk intake remains relatively constant between one and six months of age. This is based upon current research, and differs from previous thinking that breastmilk intake increased steadily in proportion to a baby's age and weight.

- Of course all babies have different needs, but the typical range of breastmilk intake is between nineteen and thirty ounces in a twenty-four-hour period for an exclusively breastfed baby.

- Sometime after six months, babies' breastmilk intake decreases gradually as solids are introduced and slowly increased.

- Remember that breastmilk (or formula) should provide the majority of babies' nutrition throughout the first year of life.

- During growth spurts which occur during the first twelve months of life, babies usually nurse or take a bottle more often than usual, and may act fussier than usual. According to the textbooks, growth spurts typically occur around seven to ten days, two to three weeks, four to six weeks, and at months three, four, six, and nine . . . but again, all babies are unique.

Source: Medela, Kellymom.com

STAND PROUD

As we learned in childbirth class, breastfeeding is all about supply and demand. The more you nurse (or pump), the more you will produce. What they forgot to tell us, though, is that some women naturally produce milk abundantly while others squeak by. Try to trust that your body will respond to your baby's appetite. Lots of Milk Mamas work full time outside the home and produce enough milk to breast-feed for a year with no formula. Other Mamas might need to supplement. The thing to remember is that *any* amount of breastmilk is good. Whether you pump one ounce or thir-teen, the fact is that it's the best food on earth. Stand proud and know that your breastmilk is giving your baby the best possible foundation for good health now and improved well-ness throughout her life. According to the American Acad-emy of Pediatrics, "When it comes to feeding babies, there is *nothing* as good as breastmilk." Of course the benefits don't stop with your baby. You get to go up a bra size, burn six hundred calories sitting still, stave off your "monthly visitor," *and* reduce your risk of breast and reproductive or-gan cancers and osteoporosis! Who can say no to all that?!

MAKING MORE

For "low flow" Mamas, we *know* it is stressful. We had a friend who was convinced her daughter would be in second grade by the time she reached twenty pounds and was able to face forward in a car seat. Lots of Mamas wonder what they've done to deserve a couple of Milk Duds. At every checkup, they pray that their babies will weigh in above the 5th percentile. Working moms have the added challenge of trying to maintain supply with a mechanical pump instead of the real thing. One working Mama summed it up by saying, "If only I could be home with my baby where the 'booby buffet' is always open, I know I would make more!"

Don't obsess. There are a number of ways to boost your supply:

- *Get plenty of rest*—ha! Really, forget that load of laundry and the phone call you need to make; go to sleep right after putting your baby down for the night.

- *Don't get stressed out*—ha ha! Yes, we know: as a working mom of an infant, stress is as unavoidable as the poopy diaper that occurs just as you're racing out the door to day care. Make it a point to relax throughout the day. Even if it's just breathing deeply with your eyes closed for a couple minutes—you can always imagine you're taking a luxurious bubble bath.

- *Invest in a high-quality, efficient pump.* Take our advice and splurge. The right pump makes a big difference. (See page 50).
- *Pump and nurse as frequently as you can.* Keep that milk mooooooooving!
  - *When you're with your baby, nurse on demand.* Despite our advice about resting, you may decide it's worth it to succumb to your baby's cries for milk in the middle of the night, even though your friends and/or inlaws insist she should be sleeping through the night by eight months or so. Some Milk Mamas find 3:00 A.M. to be a snuggly, peaceful, quiet time to bond with their babies *and* keep their milk supply up.
  - *Try pumping right after you nurse your baby.* We know that extra pumping does *not* appeal, but this is a great way to tell your breasts in no uncertain terms that your baby needs more milk!
  - *Pump at least twice a day at work.* Lactation consultants and experienced Milk Mamas agree that a nursing baby is more efficient than a breastpump, so it's important that you remain diligent about pumping as frequently as possible at work to keep up with your baby's consumption.

- *While pumping, visualize your baby.* Think of it as fantasizing Milk Mama style! Remember Mother Nature designed you with a physiological reflex that can trigger milk letdown when you just think about your baby (or sometimes when you hear another baby crying in the supermarket). Look at your baby's picture. Or close your eyes and imagine his sweet, warm mouth in place of the plastic funnel on your breast, his soft breathing in place of the breastpump motor. Your milk will let down faster, you will make a little more, and you will feel more relaxed.

- *Gently massage your breasts as you pump.* Or, have your husband do this (just kidding)! This stimulates letdown, and may also ward off clogged ducts.

- *Hunch over as you pump.* Let gravity help. You can worry about posture another day.

- *Drink plenty of water* (at least eight eight-ounce glasses or two liters per day). Most lactation experts say this doesn't directly boost milk supply, but all the Milk Mamas we know swear by it.

- *Try teas or herbal supplements containing fenugreek.* You can find "Mother's Milk" tea or fenugreek capsules at most health food stores, and even some regular grocery stores. Many moms report increased milk production after one to three days. As with all herbal supplements, proceed with caution. Fenugreek is on the U.S. Food and Drug Administration's GRAS (Generally Recognized As Safe) list when taken in moderation by nursing moms. Innocuous side effects include sweat and urine that smell like maple syrup—or a baby that smells like maple. Fenugreek is in the same family as peanuts, so don't use it if you have a peanut allergy. Also, if fenugreek causes you and/or your baby to have upset stomach or diarrhea, discontinue use. Though it's fine to use fenugreek for several weeks or even months, you will probably find that once your supply is increased, you can easily maintain it on your own by following the other advice listed here.

- *Call a lactation consultant.* Their mission is to get breastmilk into the mouths of babies, and they would love nothing more than to help you boost your supply and continue nursing happily.

- *Drink a beer*—really! Nobody is sure why, but some experts believe the hops and/or brewer's yeast stimulate milk production. Non-alcoholic beer has the same effect, but if you choose the real stuff, wait at least two hours before nursing, and note that moderation is recommended!

Friday, May 25

Ladies,

If you must know, I'm a D cup. But actually, there's no correlation between milk production and cup size. I had my share of milk-supply problems when Colby was a baby as I was recovering from mastitis (that's a whole different story!). I tried the Mother's Milk tea that contains the herb fenugreek. It boosted my production, but only after I drank a bunch of it pretty regularly. It tastes OK despite the funky licorice-maple aroma. After I had been drinking it religiously for several days, during a rare moment of intimacy my husband paused and said, "Babe, your underarm smells like a *pancake*!!" So much for the romance and candlelight!

Gotta go—I'm supposed to be in a meeting that started five minutes ago.

Jugs

P.S. I must correct the record: it was actually 13½ ounces!

Friday, May 25

That is hilarious!

I'm craving IHOP now.

Yippee—it's a three-day weekend! Happy Memorial Day.

I'm going to nurse little Charlotte all weekend long! And I just might shred my milk production log!

Cate

P.S. All I have to say about 13½ ounces is . . . MOO! ·

Tuesday, May 29

Hope everyone had a good long weekend!

Cate,

Even if you don't shred the milk log, try not to get stressed out about your supply. You're exactly right to nurse frequently when you're with Charlotte. And when you're here in the Milk Mama Clubhouse, there's a NEW RULE: don't even *think* about the meeting you're about to go to or the million things you have to do. This is your time to relax and be a MOM.

~~Stacy~~ Jugs

Tuesday, May 29

Relax?! With my breasts attached to this contraption? Sorry, I just can't seem to get there. I mean, it's only slightly better than being trapped in my office with Dirk. At least you guys (the notebook, I mean) provide some advice and humor. I know I don't always write, but I do always read what you write. By the way, when is the home entertainment system going to get here?

Steph

Tuesday, May 29

Jugs,

I'm abiding by your new rule. I'm also trying a new hunching technique that a lactation consultant told me about. Picture me now at this ridiculous brown table totally hunched over, breasts between my knees, holding the suction cups on my breasts with one hand while I write in our journal with the other. If you walked in right now you would crack up. Hey—I think it's working—over 4.5 ounces!

Cate

P.S. Steph, look at the bright side: You make 28 ounces a day, aren't worried about supply, and don't have to hunch!

Tuesday, May 29

Hmmmm . . . who's the new mom? Mystery pump under the table. Join the Milk Mama Club! WELCOME!

Andrea

Tuesday, May 29

Would you believe I just ran out of room in my bottles? 20+ ounces in two pumping sessions! Think there's a market for this stuff??

Stacy

Tuesday, May 29

Hi. My name's Anne, owner of the mystery pump. I wasn't sure if I should invite myself to join your journal group—it's very cool, by the way.

I have a 7-week-old son, Ryan (plus a 4-year-old daughter, Ella). I work at a help desk in Bldg. 24 supporting external clients. I have to find someone to answer my phone every time I leave to pee or pump.

I can relate to milk-supply woes! I only pumped a pitiful 1.5 ounces plus a smidge just now (every drop counts!). I'm constantly worried about this because Ryan is only in the 10th percentile for weight.

Anne

Wednesday, May 30

Hi Anne,

Welcome to the club. Don't worry, the hazing isn't all that bad.

Steph (Darren's mom)

Wednesday, May 30

Welcome Anne—please write in the journal anytime you're here—the more the merrier! And bring pics of Ryan and Ella!

My son Caleb is below the 5th percentile. At his last checkup/immunization (which I HATE), our pediatrician (male) said, and I quote, "You just need to get this baby some groceries." WHAT???

Stacy,

I can't believe 20+ ounces!

Sigh,

Andrea

Wednesday, May 30

CALL THE LA LECHE LEAGUE! CALL THE GUINNESS BOOK OF WORLD RECORDS! STACY, YOU ARE A FREAK OF NATURE! I mean that as a compliment, of course. You know, a hundred years ago, you could have had a very promising career as a wet nurse! Some days, I would prefer that to this stressful IBM job.

Cate

P.S. Welcome, Anne! I'm Charlotte's mom.

P.P.S. Andrea, immunizations are the *worst*. I always feel terrible when Charlotte is sitting happily on my lap smiling at the nurse, who then pokes her with a needle! I try to warn Charlotte that it's coming, and explain that I'm doing it because I love her and don't want her to get sick—as if she can understand what I'm saying! We both end up in tears. By the way, does your doctor know that four-month-old babies don't eat *groceries*? They eat *breastmilk*, which is why we're here!!! Good Lord.

> *Wednesday, May 30*
>
> I saw in the paper there's a walk to benefit La Leche League next weekend. Stacy, you should be the Grand Marshall!
>
> Andrea

Note: See page 352 for a sample Milk Mama Production Log.

A MATTER OF TIMING

> *Monday, June 4*
>
> Here's my newest problem: I always end up pumping later in the afternoon than I had planned. Then I worry that I'll pump too much, and when I finally get home to cuddle with Charlotte and nurse her, the well will be dry! ☹
>
> Cate

Monday, June 4

Cate,

I TOTALLY know what you mean about pumping too much in the afternoon. I always seem to find myself pumping after 4:00. I know I have to pump so that Caleb has enough milk for the following day, but I hate the thought of returning home and worrying that he is not getting enough milk from me in the evening. Right now it's 4:55 and I'm trying to speed-pump in 5 minutes because I can't be late to pick up Caleb tonight. On top of work stress, we're MILK stressed!

Andrea

Tuesday, June 5

Here's a positive thought for you low-flow Mamas: when your babies nurse hungrily after you get home from work, they're actually telling your body to produce more milk. Over time this should boost your supply.

Moooooo!

Stacy

Tuesday, June 5

I'm glad to know that I'm not the only one who struggles with time management and milk supply. I get fined $1 (per kid!) for every minute I'm late to pick up Ella and Ryan at day care. (They go to an in-home day care in our neighborhood.) There is a big red clock right at the entrance, and I swear it's three minutes fast. I'm a single mom, so drop-off and pickup (plus spit-up, clean-up, wake-up, pack-up) are all up to me.

Anne

Tuesday, June 5

Wow, Anne. Didn't realize you were a single mom! I can't imagine. I feel like I can barely handle this juggling act, and I have a super-helpful husband and tons of family in town. I hope you have some support. It sounds like the father of your kids is not involved (don't mean to be nosy). Feel free to vent (or brag) here whenever you want!

Andrea

Wednesday, June 6

Well, Ella's dad left me before her first birthday. Turns out he was having an affair with a Starbucks barista the whole time. He wants nothing to do with Ella or me, which is sad, but probably for the best—you can't force someone to be a loving father (or husband). Ryan is the product of a wild fling and a faulty condom. His dad is an artist in Santa Fe. We keep in touch, he pays some child support, and he's going to try to visit several times a year. He's a really good guy, but I could never see us spending more than one week in the same house, never mind getting married. We're just too different.

So, I've given up on romance, at least for now. My kids are the loves of my life.

Anne

Wednesday, June 6

Oh Anne, what a hard road you've traveled. God bless you. The only job in the world harder than motherhood is single-motherhood. I really admire you for pulling it off. Of course we could never substitute for a dad, but you can always count on us Milk Mamas for support and a few good laughs.

Cate

There's no doubt about it, establishing and sticking to a regular pumping schedule while you're at work is a challenge. Despite your best intentions, there will be days when you find yourself racing against the clock to pump enough milk for the following day while making sure there's enough left to feed your baby when you get home. Try to finish your second pumping session several hours before you go home. When this is not possible, don't stress. Just pump a little less than usual and make tomorrow a "dip into savings" day.

MIXING FRESH, FROZEN, AND FORMULA: RECIPES FOR SUCCESS

Wednesday, June 6

Hi again. Quick question: since I'm a low-flow Mama, can I combine freshly pumped breastmilk with thawed frozen breastmilk? Or even formula? I can't imagine ever producing the 30 ounces Stacy's doctor recommended. (That's almost enough breastmilk to fill a Big Gulp cup!)

Drip drip,

Anne

You've tried everything to boost your supply—you've hunched over and begged gravity to open the floodgates, you've massaged your breasts and willed them to fill up like water balloons, you've pumped until smoke is billowing from your breastpump. And it's still not enough. Now what? Should you dip into your frozen stockpile? Or is now the time to start supplementing with formula? There is no simple answer. It depends on how low your production is, the amount of milk in your freezer, and whether or not you're a purist when it comes to breastmilk versus formula.

Some low-flow Mamas can't imagine feeding their babies anything but breastmilk for the first year—and sure enough, their bodies produce what their babies need. Despite their worries about supply, their babies gain weight and are perfectly healthy. When their daily pumping doesn't produce quite enough, they reluctantly go to the freezer for a small ration of frozen breastmilk.

The recipe for mixing milk is simple. You can combine breastmilk from different pumping sessions, frozen or fresh. You can also add freshly pumped milk to refrigerated milk. Ideally the fresh milk should be cooled to the same temperature as the refrigerated milk first. Just remember that once you combine milk, its freshness is tied to the oldest vintage. Say you combine milk from a Monday and a Wednesday— then all the milk is as if it were pumped on Monday.

Some moms find producing enough milk simply impossible. Some just need to be freed from constantly worrying about milk supply. These moms supplement with formula. It's fine to mix formula with breastmilk, fresh or thawed. But it's ideal to offer them separately—breastmilk first, then formula if needed. This way any unfinished portion (which purists would tell you to discard) is less likely to be precious breastmilk. If you choose to do this, remember this caution: once you begin to supplement, the natural supply-and-demand process of breastmilk production can get thrown off. So keep pumping and nursing!

And don't let yourself or any one else make you feel guilty or inadequate for using formula. The fact that you're breastfeeding at all while working is a true accomplishment.

FRESH (AND NOT SO FRESH) MILK

There's nothing worse than pouring unused breastmilk down the drain. After all the time and care you invested in pumping, how can you send your precious milk to mingle with the scraps from last night's dinner? One Milk Mama couldn't figure out why her baby was continually crying and pushing the bottle away during feedings. After taking a whiff of the milk, she solved the mystery (and felt horrible for trying to feed her baby something that smelled like dirty feet). After that, she began writing expiration dates on her frozen and fresh milk bags. To avoid this tragedy, know how to keep your milk fresh.

breastmilk storage, thawing, and warming guidelines

STORAGE:

- Freshly pumped milk stays good for up to ten hours at room temperature.

- Fresh milk can be stored in a cooler with ice packs for up to twenty-four hours.
- Refrigerated breastmilk is good for up to eight days. It's a good idea to store the milk in the back of the refrigerator instead of in the door.
- Frozen breastmilk lasts three to four months in a freezer, depending on how often you open the door to get some ice cream. Your best bet is to store the milk in the back of the freezer. Or you can buy a chest-type freezer, where frozen breastmilk can be stored for up to six months or longer. If you have a freezer compartment (rather than a freezer with a separate door), the frozen milk must be used within two weeks.
- It's best to use bags specifically designed for storing human milk. They are thick, presterilized, and lined with nylon to prevent fat from adhering to the sides. (Too bad there's no material like that for our thighs!)
- Thawed breastmilk must be used within twenty-four hours. Once thawed, breastmilk should not be refrozen.
- It's not known whether milk from an unfinished bottle can be safely reused or if it should be poured down the sink (gasp!).

THAWING AND WARMING:
- Thaw breastmilk in the refrigerator, which takes about twelve hours.
- Don't thaw breastmilk at room temperature because of poten-

tial temperature fluctuations, which may affect the freshness of
the milk.

- Also, don't thaw breastmilk in the microwave (which can create hot spots), or in extremely hot water (which can decrease
the milk's antibodies).
- For faster thawing, and to warm breastmilk to serving temperature, hold the container of milk under warm running water, or
submerge it in a bowl of warm water.

Source: La Leche League

The La Leche League guidelines above have changed
over the years, so don't listen to the "expert" mother of
three who is bound to tell you that you must throw away all
frozen breastmilk after two months! Although the La Leche
League guidelines aren't specific on whether or not you can
reuse unfinished milk, one small study suggests it is safe to
reuse milk within one or two hours. Also, in the real world,
most Mamas we know have thawed breastmilk at room temperature, carrying a few ounces of frozen milk in their diaper bags and letting it thaw over a few hours. Generally
speaking, like grocery store cow's milk, if it smells or tastes
bad it probably is bad; otherwise it's probably fine.

Sadly, we knew a few Milk Mamas whose milk always
seemed to spoil quickly. They had too much of an enzyme
called lipase, which breaks down fats in human milk. They

could only store their milk for eight to ten hours in the refrigerator before it started smelling and tasting funky. If you have this problem, you can stop the breakdown of fat by scalding your milk before storing it. This involves heating the milk until it bubbles and removing it from the burner before it boils. Of course, this presents an obvious hurdle during the work hours. Can't you just see yourself now, lugging a portable Coleman stove to work so that you can cook your breastmilk between meetings? If you think you may have this lipase problem, consult with a certified lactation consultant.

DON'T WORRY, BE HOPPY!

Thursday, June 7

Great news for the weekend!! This just in: I heard that drinking a *beer* a day can improve milk supply! I don't know if it's true, but I volunteer to experiment!

Cate

Thursday, June 7

I forgot about the beer thing. I heard that too when I was struggling with milk supply for Colby. I heard it has something to do with the hops or brewer's yeast, which is also available in capsule or powder form in health food stores. But I'm all for the beer idea. I asked my pediatrician if drinking a beer was OK while breastfeeding. She of course quoted the American Academy of Pediatrics breastmilk policy statement. It's very specific regarding alcohol—I'll look it up and write it in the journal tomorrow. . . .

Stacy

Thursday, June 7

Here's to hops! I'm not having supply problems, but I'm still going to call my husband and tell him to have a frosty mug waiting for me when I get home (another bonus to having a stay-at-home dad).

Steph

Friday, June 8

OK, here's the policy statement, and I quote: "An *occasional celebratory single, small* alcoholic drink is acceptable, but breastfeeding should be avoided for two hours after the drink."

Do you think a pony keg would be acceptable? Let's bring one into our Milk Mama Clubhouse. If it doesn't increase our milk supply, at least we won't care anymore.

Stacy

nanny 911

Monday, June 11

When I dropped Ryan and Ella off at JoAnne's (day-care lady) this morning, there was a "FOR SALE" sign in her yard! For a quick second, I thought I was at the wrong house . . . but no such luck. The sign just went up this morning and JoAnne hadn't had time to warn all the parents yet. Her husband got transferred and they are moving in a month. I need to go on an emergency day-care search. Do you guys know of anything? Why me?

Anne

Monday, June 11

I wish I could tell you where to go, but I rely on my aunt and my mom to watch Caleb when I'm in the office Mon–Wed, and my neighbor helps for a couple hours in the mornings on Thurs–Fri when I work from home. The busier Caleb gets, the harder it's becoming for me to get work done on those days. Last week he entertained me for an hour rolling over onto his tummy, arching his back with his shoulders and legs off the ground and arms straight out—a little airplane ready for takeoff!

So . . . I'll probably be looking for Thurs–Fri day care myself before too long. I'm already dreading leaving Caleb with a stranger.

Andrea

Tuesday, June 12

Clearly, what we *all* need is to win the lottery. When is the IBM sundry shop going to start selling lottery tickets?

Show me the MOOOOLA,

Cate

P.S. Charlotte hated tummy time, so she never mastered the "airplane."

Tuesday, June 12

Anne,

George and Colby go to an awesome in-home day care in Longmont (don't you live there, too?). It's great—I love it! I think she has a waiting list, but I'll check.

Stacy

P.S. Colby also hated tummy time! He was *always* on his back, and I swear his head is still flat in back because of it.

Tuesday, June 12

If you get in a real pinch, I could ask my husband, Chad, to watch Ella and Ryan for a few days until you find a new place. He'll have Ella painting like Picasso in no time. Hey—we need some new artwork for this room! Do you think IBM would mind if we took the '80s Family Day poster out of the frame and replaced it with colorful kid art?

Steph

Tuesday, June 12

Steph,

Thanks for the offer. If I get desperate, I may take you up on it. As for the art, I'm all for cheerier decor in here. I could bring in one of Ryan's dad's paintings. They're amazing.

Stacy, yes—I live in Longmont. Please do check with your day-care person. Thanks!

Anne

Tuesday, June 12

Anne,

The only thing I have experience with is a nanny. It costs a fortune, but I do love knowing Charlotte is home with either the nanny or my husband every day. No diaper bag to pack, no drop-off/pickup, milk mix-ups, green-boogered kids . . . and she gets to sleep in her own crib and play with her own toys. But forget saving for college—I feel like we're pouring all our money into our nanny's checking account. We don't have any family in the area, but I'm trying to bribe my mother-in-law to move here (desperation).

Cate

P.S. To make a nanny affordable, maybe you could share one with another family. We have friends who do that. The nanny watches both kids full-time, alternating houses week to week.

Wednesday, June 13

Anne,

I checked with my day-care lady and unfortunately she's full (I mean her day care). I went ahead and put your name on the waitlist—hope that's OK.

Stacy

Wednesday, June 13

Thanks for all the ideas. I made appointments with a couple day-care places. I don't think I can afford a nanny, even shared. I'll let you know how it goes.

Anne

THE GOOD-BYE KISS

Every mom who works outside the home has to face the day she leaves her baby with someone else. When this day comes for you, it may help to realize that there are thousands of other moms doing the exact same thing that morning. They too are waking up with a hollow feeling in the pit of their stomach, worrying about how their babies will do without them, and how they will get through their first day back at work. You are not alone. Leaving your baby on that first day is one of the hardest things all new working moms do. Over time you'll get into a routine, but it doesn't mean that walking away is ever easy. Whether it's the first time or the hundredth, that "Good-bye, Mommy loves you" kiss will tug at your heart.

Adding to the difficulty is the negative portrayal of day care by everyone from the national media to your mother-in-law. Just when you're feeling halfway comfortable with your day-care arrangement, you hear a story about a lice breakout in a day-care center, a nanny caught on hidden camera neglecting or shaking a baby, or a family member molesting or physically abusing a child. It's enough to make any parent apprehensive, to say the least. The truth is that millions of families have positive day-care experiences. Children are safe, generally happy, learning to interact with others, and still maintaining a strong bond with their parents. But the happy stories aren't front-page news. Of course you will be meticulously choosy and observant when it comes to your child's safety and well-being, but don't let yourself become paralyzed by fear. You will find good day care. We have yet to meet a Milk Mama who hasn't . . . if not right away, eventually.

Monday, June 18

Progress report on day-care search: door number 1: In-home day care—home was pretty much a wreck. Smelled like rotten eggs and poopy diapers. The TV was blaring, the kids were running wild and had Kool-Aid mustaches. I ruled the place out within 30 seconds, but the lady, Mrs. Crownover (what a name), insisted on giving me a tour. In the basement she explained that she didn't let the kids play near the furnace, and to "prevent" them from getting too close, she had an old couch pushed up against it. Like that's going to keep the kids away? Will keep you in suspense for door number 2.

Anne

P.S. Hope your families enjoyed Father's Day. It's always a weird day for me. Ryan cooed into the phone for his dad. I dread having to explain the whole thing to him someday. Ella asked to call her daddy, too, but he didn't answer the phone. I told her that we'd try to find a new daddy for her someday. It would be nice if that came true.

Monday, June 18

Anne,

You'll find the right man if that's what you want. In the meantime, I am so impressed by your ability to manage a household, a career, and two kids on your own.

I'm so sorry you're in this day-care crisis—what a pain!

When I was looking for day care after Colby was born, I walked into a center without an appointment (a good way to check a place out). The front door wasn't locked, so I opened it and peeked in—to find a room full of sleeping children, and no adult in sight! Hello??!!! Then there was the time that a dog bit my husband during an in-home day-care tour. Don't mean to freak you out. We did end up finding a great place, and so will you!

Stacy

Monday, June 18

Anne,

I don't know whether you're also looking at day-care centers, but here's something to check out if you are. My friend couldn't believe it when she learned that the security code which unlocks the front door (1) matched the street address of the building, and (2) never changed. It wouldn't take much of a sleuth to crack that code! Sheesh.

Hang in there—you'll find something.

C

P.S. Who still drinks Kool-Aid?

Monday, June 18

Serenity now!!! Stop with the horror stories! When I start to look for day care, this is going to give me nightmares.

Andrea

P.S. Caleb update: we celebrated his 5-month birthday by giving him rice cereal this weekend! Most of it ended up on his face, but it made for great pictures!

Monday, June 18

Andrea,

Watch out for sneezes!

Door number 2: The place seemed really nice, but already had 4 kids. 2 more would still be a legal adult-to-child ratio, but still it seemed like my kids might get ignored. How is one person going to pay attention to 6 kids?

Door number 3: $1,500/month. Good-bye.

Anne

Monday, June 18

What is with these day cares? And why is it so hard for some of them to give parents peace of mind? That should be their mission in life, especially when a new mom is coming to visit. Turn off the TV, wipe the kids' faces, and have them playing duck-duck-goose. Explain the daily schedule and show that you know *something* about child development and safety. And even if the little girl looks like Mr. Potato Head, pick her up, smile at her, and say, "You're so beautiful!"

I'm forever grateful to Chad for putting his career on hold to take care of Darren. I'm keeping my fingers crossed for you, Anne, and remember, we can back you up in a pinch!

Steph

Wednesday, June 20

Took yesterday off to search. I'll spare you the details of doors 4 through 8. You'll be glad to know that I found The One behind door number 9. She totally connected with Ryan and Ella, had an obvious love of children, a calm, clean environment, and was tuned in to the kids there. She stopped several times during the interview to change a diaper, pick up a baby, and answer one of the kid's questions. I had a good feeling about the place.

Whew! The kids will start going there the second week in July.

Anne

P.S. Stephanie, tell Chad he's off the hook—and thanks!

SEEKING MARY POPPINS

Rule number one when it comes to choosing a day-care provider is that you must find someone you trust. But how can you trust a person whom you've just met? After all, it's not as if you're asking them to watch your suitcase while you run to the restroom. You are entrusting your baby—your very heart and soul—to the care of another. Will this person soothe your baby the way you would? Will they know how to calm her when she's upset? Will they give her the attention she needs and deserves? Will your baby be happy during the day? Will they notice when her diaper is wet? Will they connect with her? These questions are normal. You may find yourself overwhelmed by them as you visit several people/places. Of course, nobody can ever take the place of mommy or daddy. Even so, your child can enjoy a positive, loving experience while you are at work. Your job is to find the person or people who can provide that good experience, for you and your baby.

As you go about your search, always listen to and trust your intuition. If you have even the slightest notion that something isn't right, move on. While there's no such thing as trust at first sight, you'll have an easier time building trust if you have a good feeling to start with.

It might help you to remember that most people who have chosen day care as their profession certainly didn't choose it as a way to get rich, they chose it because they have a natural love of children. While you may feel fearful, unsure, and uneasy about the prospect of finding someone to watch your child, know that the process will be easier if you approach it with an open mind and a positive attitude.

FINANCIAL FOREWARNING

Now that your mind is open (right?), prepare yourself for the outrageous cost of child care. According to the National Association of Child Care Resource and Referral Agencies, in most areas of the United States, child care expenses come close to or exceed housing costs. In forty-two states, the cost for infant care exeeds tuition at a four-year public university. Think of it as a new tithe—the average family spends more than 10 percent of their annual household income on infant care. Single parents fork over more than 30 percent! Clearly, these facts illustrate a working parent's dilemma. After subtracting the cost of day care from your net income, is it still worth it to continue working? Of course, you also have to factor in benefits, your career path, and how satisfying your work is. If you decide to keep working, your next decision is who will take care of your little one—and how much your pocketbook can bear.

Average Cost of Child Care Per Year

	LOW	HIGH
Licensed In-home Care[*]	$2,200	$13,100
Child-Care Center[†]	$3,800	$13,500
Au Pair	$14,400	$18,500
Nanny (live-in)	$20,000	$31,000
Nanny (live-out)	$26,000	$36,400

Sources: National Association of Child Care Resource and Referral Agencies;
Au Pair in America; NannyLocators.com
[*]Average cost of infant or toddler care
[†]Average cost of infant care

HOME SWEET HOME

One of the first places many parents want to leave their babies is in their own homes. Having a nanny come to your house is very convenient. You don't have to pack your baby up each morning or remove him from his familiar surroundings. If your baby gets sick, he can stay at home with the nanny, and you won't have to miss a day of work. On the other hand, if your nanny gets sick, you'll either need to stay home or have a backup plan. Another drawback to in-home care is the expense. Whether nannies are paid by the hour or are salaried, they typically cost significantly more than other options. Also, the IRS requires you and your nanny to pay Social Security (FICA) and Medicare taxes on any amount earned over $1,500 per year. In addition, you must pay federal and state unemployment insurance, and other state and local taxes. When all is said and done, your tax cost (as the employer) will add up to about 10 percent of your nanny's gross pay. On top of this, your nanny will have to pay income taxes. When these are included, the total hit to your nanny's take-home pay will be about 20 percent (e.g., $373 per week instead of $465). You can withhold income taxes from your nanny's pay, or your nanny can pay them quarterly. The good news is that there is a federal dependent-care assistance program that enables you to use up to $5,000 in pretax earnings to pay for child care. Depending on your income, you may also qualify for a tax credit of 20 to 35 percent of child care expenses. You may also be expected to give paid vacation time and/or sick days. One way to reduce the expense is to share a nanny with another family. The nanny will make more while you pay less, and your baby will enjoy interacting with other children. You'll need to find a family who has similar values and compatible kids, and with whom you foresee having a long-term relationship. From there, you can work out the details of pay, schedule, and location.

If there's extra room in your house, you might also consider hiring an au pair. Au pairs come from all regions of the world and are usually in their early twenties. They are recruited by U.S. agencies to live with American families for up to two years. Once you apply for an au pair, you get to interview candidates via phone and e-mail who meet your criteria (country of origin, age range, English proficiency, smoker/nonsmoker, years of child-care experience) and select the person who best matches the needs of your family. There is an upfront agency fee of $6,000 to $10,000, which covers travel, orientation/training, health insurance, and tax. Once she arrives, the au pair can work up to forty-five hours per week and gets paid about $150 per week. This option costs less than hiring a nanny but usually more than traditional day care. Besides keeping your child in your own home, he will learn about another culture as he grows and might even be introduced to a foreign language. The scary thing is hiring someone sight unseen. You can trade e-mails and pictures and talk on the phone, but you still have to reach a decision without meeting in person. Of course, the agency interviews every candidate locally and provides a thorough orientation. If the match doesn't work out, there are provisions for "rematching." The first few weeks after the au pair arrives is a time of adjustment for everyone, so if you choose this option and encounter problems, try to give it four to six weeks before asking for a rematch (unless she's a kleptomaniac who serves Twinkies for breakfast, lunch, and dinner).

ALL IN THE FAMILY

If you are fortunate enough to live near your family, you might be able to rely on them for child care. Grandparents, aunts, and uncles can help ease the worry of entrusting your baby to another. After all, you've known them all your life, and they already have a relationship with your little one and look forward to spending time with him. Best of all, the price is right. For this arrangement to succeed, everyone must be open about expectations and concerns. Grandparents need to speak up if they feel taken advantage of, and parents need to feel comfortable voicing any issues. If you can achieve this, the result will be a deeper relationship and an everlasting bond.

adult-to-child ratio: what's best?

- The ideal adult-to-child ratio for an infant (6 weeks to 18 months) is no more than 1 to 4. Currently, 36 states mandate this ratio. Several states (such as California, Kansas, Maryland, and Massachusetts) do better than this, mandating a ratio of 1 to 3.

    Unfortunately, some states (Arkansas, Georgia, Idaho, Louisiana, and Nevada) are behind the times and allow a ratio of 1 to 7.

- As your child gets older, ideal ratios change. The ideal ratio for a 4-year-old is no more than 1 to 10. Twenty states mandate this. California and New York require an even healthier ratio of 1 to 8, while states such as North Carolina and Florida allow 1 to 20! Can you imagine single-handedly watching 20 energy-charged 4-year-olds?

Source: National Association of Child Care Resource and Referral Agencies

NEIGHBORLY LOVE

Another option, still in a home environment, is taking your baby to an in-home day care. Look for someone who is licensed by the state, which helps ensure that the home is safe for children and that the provider isn't an ax murderer. A licensed home is also required to stay within the state-mandated child-to-adult ratio. The best way to find an in-home day care is word of mouth. Ask other working parents where they take their children. You'll feel better getting the scoop from someone you know rather than from a

Average Cost of Child Care Per Year
(for licensed child-care centers)

	INFANT	PRESCHOOL AGE (FOUR-YEAR-OLD)
Lowest Sample States	$3,800 to $4,400 Alabama, Arkansas, Nevada, Mississippi	$3,000 to $4,000 Alabama, Nevada, Arkansas, West Virginia
Midrange Sample States	$6,300 to $7,000 Florida, Oregon, Iowa, Ohio	$4,800 to $5,500 Idaho, Iowa, Indiana, Wyoming
Highest Sample States	$10,300 to $13,500 Connecticut, New Jersey, Minnesota Massachusetts	$8,500 to $10,000 New York, Minnesota New Jersey, Massachusetts

Source: National Association of Child Care Resource and Referral Agencies

reference on a list, who will generally have only positive things to say. Failing word of mouth, you can request a list of licensed in-home care providers through your local Child-Care Resource and Referral (CCR&R) organization. Find a provider who matches what you want for your child, whether that is a structured learning environment or a place where the emphasis is on having fun and catching crawdads in a creek.

DON'T FORGET DAY CARE

There is always the option of a traditional day-care center. These range from chaotic drop-off centers to full-fledged educational academies, including specialized schools such as Montessori or Waldorf. The main benefit of day-care centers is that you can generally count on them to be open and staffed—no last-minute scrambling to find backup care when your provider goes on vacation or is sick. Speaking of sick, the main disadvantage is germs galore. You might be attracted to the convenience of a reliable day-care center, but don't forget that even with the immunity boost from breastmilk, your child is likely to get sick more often, which means that someone will need to stay home with him. Overall, if you can find a great day care, your baby will benefit from social interaction, exposure to a variety of toys, books, and learning materials, and will learn to adapt to new people and environments.

twenty questions to ask child-care providers

1. Are you certified/licensed/accredited? Providers caring for more than six or seven children are required to be licensed. Specific criteria differ by state, but in general, a licensed or certified provider has had a background check and met certain standards for safety and adult-to-child ratios. Also, they must be recertified or renew their license every few years. Accredited providers have met voluntary standards for child care that are usually higher than state requirements.

2. What education do you and your staff have?

3. What is the adult-to-child ratio?

4. Do you have first-aid training? Are you certified in infant and child CPR?

5. What is your policy regarding sick kids? Do you send kids home at the first hint of a sniffle, or do you wait until a child has a fever? You'll need to know when to get backup care for your child, and you'll also want reassurance that all parents will be asked to keep their green-boogered kids at home.

6. Do I have to pay for days when my child is absent due to sickness or vacation? Usually, the answer is yes, but some care facilities allow for a week or two of vacation time per year. Some will give you a break if your child has an extended illness.

7. How do you discipline children when you see tantrums, push-ing, fighting, and arguments? It's important to find out which discipline methods are used as well as which ones are prohibited. Ask your provider to put their discipline practices into writing.

8. What would you do if my baby cried inconsolably?

9. How much do you charge if I'm late to pick up my child? It's common for child-care providers to charge one dollar for every minute you're late. However, some have a "three-strike" policy—only after the third time you're late will you have to get out your wallet.

10. Can I make unannounced visits to see/observe my child? Stay away from any provider who doesn't allow you to come and go or that has a strict visiting schedule. You should al-ways feel welcome to observe your child during the day.

11. How will my child be checked in and out each day? What would you do if my child fell? Do you practice fire drills? How would you handle an emergency situation (earthquake, tornado, national security threat)?

12. What is your staff turnover rate? Turnover at day-care cen-ters averages 30 to 40 percent per year, but you can find a cen-ter that has a lower rate.

13. What is a typical day like? Make sure the answer you get matches what you're looking for in an in-home or day-care center, whether that be a structured daily routine or a free-flowing atmosphere.

14. What do you like most about caring for infants/children?

What do you like least? Why did you decide to become a child-care provider?

15. On which holidays do you close? Is there a backup provider? If you are interviewing an in-home provider, it's also a good idea to find out what happens when she is sick or on vacation. Many providers make arrangements with another in-home provider in the neighborhood who can care for your child. If this is the case, make sure you meet the backup provider as well.

16. Do you drive the children anywhere? If yes, ask to see the vehicle and car seats.

17. Do you smoke? Do you have pets?

18. How much notice is needed if I decide to switch day cares?

19. What is your billing policy? Do you provide receipts for income tax credits?

20. Will you give me a list of references?

THE BRIGHT SIDE

Monday, June 25

Did everyone enjoy the weekend?

Congratulations, Anne! I'm so happy that you found a place—it sounds great. I knew it would work out.

Stacy

Monday, June 25

Hooray, Anne! You of all people deserve reliable, stress-free child care.

Andrea

Monday, June 25

What a relief, Anne! I'll sleep better, too. I've totally been thinking about you!

Sorry to take away from the celebration, but I'm having a bit of a child-care crisis myself. No, my nanny didn't quit (Thank God) (or maybe not?). . . . I'm just obsessed with the question of *why* I am paying my nanny so much money to be with Charlotte, which is where *I* want to be, but instead I am here doing a job I don't even like that much. So I can make money . . . to pay the nanny. It makes me crazy and sad. I can't think about it too much.

Cate

Monday, June 25

Cate,

I know what you mean! Sometimes I wonder about working parents having other people help raise their children. My neighbors have a full-time nanny and I see her with the kids all the time. But I haven't seen the parents since Halloween. There has to be a balance. I wouldn't feel satisfied leaving

Caleb with another person for 50 hours a week, and yet I couldn't be a full-time stay-at-home mom. For me, I think a part-time job would be the perfect answer. Let's hope my manager comes around to that.

I think the time we spend working would be easier to rationalize if we were feeding the poor or curing cancer. But we're not. I write newsletters for IBM printer salespeople to help them sell more printers to print bills and junk mail. So even though I don't have to pay for child care (yet), I spend less time with Caleb—why? So that I can help fill everyone's mailbox with stuff they don't want and/or will just throw away. Now, *that's* satisfying.

Andrea

Tuesday, June 26

Oh, just wait until your babies get a little older and begin to love day care because they spend so much time there. Sometimes when I pick up Colby and George, they cry because they don't want to leave. It's a heartbreaker.

Before we soak this spiral with tears, let's try to think of a few good things about being working moms. Come on, I know you can come up with something! I can—more later.

Stacy

Hmmm . . . like what?

Anne

Tuesday, June 26

I'll start! I like being a working mom because I really enjoy what I do. Maybe that's the key, Andrea and Cate. . . . The more your job fulfills you, the easier it is to adjust to being a working mom. I get more than a salary from my job— I get interaction with friends and mental stimulation. Plus, my career is a big part of my identity. I learned the importance of being self-sufficient from my mom. She was a social worker, and I used to love listening to stories about how she helped people. Looking back, I realize how important it is that I saw her as a multifaceted person, rather than "just" a mom (don't mean to be disrespectful, but you know what I mean, right?). I hope I can trade work stories with Darren when he gets older too, and that he will see that Chad and I are more than Mommy and Daddy.

Of course I hate missing "firsts" as much as any mom. Just yesterday Chad e-mailed me a picture of Darren reaching for the polka-dotted cow that hangs over his bouncy seat. But if I'm really honest, I think I have the best of both worlds.

Steph

Tuesday, June 26

This is a tough assignment, Stacy, but I think I've come up with something. Every week, my mom takes pictures of Caleb, prints them out, and gives them to me when I pick him up. I love looking at the pictures and seeing what he did all day. But more than that, I love having a week-by-week photo journal of him. I can really see how he's changed. This is tinged with a little sadness, of course, because I have an entire photo album of him doing things I wasn't there to see.

Andrea

Tuesday, June 26

How cool is that?! I'm going to put my nanny to work with the camera!

Let's see . . . what can I add? My nanny is an awesome guitar player and singer. She sings with Charlotte all the time—her lullabies are the best. Charlotte is mesmerized. My musical talents ended with the recorder in sixth grade.

Cate

Tuesday, June 26

Cate,

You hit the nail on the head. I think the best thing is that when we introduce our children to other people and places, it expands their world. Other caregivers do things we might never think of (or be capable of), whether that's new foods, stories, music, adventures. Tell me my kids would have ever tried quinoa at home!

Stacy

Wednesday, June 27

First of all, what's quinoa?

Anne

Wednesday, June 27

My point exactly. It's a high-protein grain that you sweeten with a little cinnamon and sugar (or honey when they're older). Another example is that my day-care provider sometimes takes all the kids to her parents' farm. She has a big van already equipped with car seats. The other day, they got to see a newborn calf. Now Colby wants one as a pet, but that's another story.

Stacy

Wednesday, June 27

Here's what I like about being a working mom. Besides providing for my children, I get a much-needed break from them—and they get to do fun things that I never seem to find time for, like crafts. I'll bring in my favorite for you to see (I'm all about putting some kid artwork in here!). Ella painted a hand-print flower (the fingers were the petals) for me for my birthday. She was so proud of it and excited to give it to me.

Anne

Wednesday, June 27

Anne,

I'm with you—having a break from my kids helps me be a better mom when I'm with them. Also, I like setting a positive example that I have gotten a good education and worked hard to get where I am. I'm proud of my work, and although I miss my kids, pursuing my career is my way of showing them that it's healthy to have multiple sources of fulfillment: family, marriage, career, hobbies. . . . And whether they ultimately choose to be stay-at-home dads or high-flying executives, it's OK. We all need to choose what's right for us.

Stacy

Wednesday, June 27

Ladies,

Here's one more working-mom bonus: fresh-baked scones from the IBM cafeteria! When's the last time you baked scones at home?

Andrea

. . .

SEVEN

sleeping like a baby

Monday, July 2

Mirror, mirror, on the wall . . . who's the tiredest mom of all? When I looked in the mirror this morning, I think a 60-year-old woman was staring back at me. She had puffy dark circles under her eyes, a skunk stripe of gray hair, and pale skin. Where did she come from? And why is my husband sleeping with her?

I have GOT to get more sleep. When did your babies start sleeping through the night?

Steph

Monday, July 2

Oh my gosh . . . that lady has been to my house too!

My little Charlotte first slept through the night about a

month ago (at 6 months), but there are still several nights a week when she wakes up crying in the middle of the night. Call me crazy—I go and nurse her back to sleep. It's like I'm in a trance. I swear someone hypnotized me, saying, "You're getting verrryyy sleepy. You are now in a deeep, deeep sleep. Every time you hear the sound of Charlotte crying in the night, you'll arise from your bed and walk down the dark hallway to her room. You will pick her up, sit in the rocking chair, and nurse Charlotte to her heart's content. There is no limit to how many times you will do this." Will our brains ever be "normal" again?

Cate

Monday, July 2

Cate,

You are so funny!

Steph,

Caleb is 5½ months (how is that possible??). Don't hate me, but he slept through the night at 7 weeks. As wonderful as that sounds, I still have to wake up to pump to keep my supply up (if I had started with a good pump, maybe I wouldn't have these supply problems). I feel like I'm never fully awake *or* fully asleep!

I almost don't remember what it feels like to wake up well rested and energized. I daydream about getting 9 hours of uninterrupted sleep, but judging by my older kids, that won't happen for another 7 years.

We're here for you.

Andrea

Monday, July 2

Stephanie,

I think we can all relate to what you're going through, especially the tiredness. Whoever coined the phrase "sleeping like a baby" obviously never had a kid! Be thankful you guys have husbands to nudge, and say, "Your turn!"

Anne, a.k.a. Sleepy

Monday, July 2

I've been through this twice (returning to work and nursing), and I promise it does get easier. Babies begin sleeping through the night at all different ages—my pediatrician always says, "There's a wide range of normal." We used the Ferber method. Stephanie, if you haven't already researched sleep-training techniques, "Ferberizing" is strict but effective. At a few months of age you begin to let the baby cry it out— you can come into the room at progressively longer time intervals (5 minutes, then 10, then 15 . . .) to reassure him briefly, but you don't pick him up. Colby learned to soothe himself to sleep within a week, so he slept through the night by the time he turned 4 months. George isn't quite there yet—probably because we've been lax on Ferberizing. Now that he's nearly 6 months, we need to get with the program.

~~Stacy~~ Doc

Tuesday, July 3

I desperately need help, too. Ryan gets up three times during the night. His loud crying wakes up Ella (my 4-year-old). She gets out of bed to "help." Then she thinks she should get a snack since Ryan's getting breastmilk. It's a regular party at 3:00 A.M. ☹ I'm ready to feed both of them (and myself) some Nyquil. When Ella was a baby, I did reach the point where I had to let her cry it out. But with Ryan, I can't do that unless I'm willing to let his crying wake up Ella. Any chance a 4-year-old would sleep in ear muffs? Ha.

Zzzzzzzzz, Anne

P.S. Anyone have fun plans for the 4th?

Tuesday, July 3

I am actually nodding off as I pump. This is ridiculous. Still, I can't imagine just letting Darren cry in the middle of the night. He would feel so confused and abandoned, and I would feel guilty lying in bed listening to him cry. I'm already gone during the day—I feel like I should at least be there for him at night. I can't ask Chad to get up because he's with Darren all day. What am I going to do?

Steph

No big plans for tomorrow, just hanging out. We're skipping fireworks. I'd rather sleep!

Tuesday, July 3

Why is it that when a dad stays home, you can't ask him to get up at night? Think of all the stay-at-home moms who are on duty day and night. Right or wrong, I don't think working dads feel the same level of guilt. They figure that because they have to get up and work the next day, they need to sleep. We're so different that sometimes I wonder why women and men choose to cohabitate. . . . Then I think about my husband Bill's adorable dimples and sexy butt and I remember why (the dimples are on his cheeks—his face, I mean)!

Stacy

Tuesday, July 3

LOL, Stacy! Maybe we should learn from men to feel a little less guilty (and they should learn from us, too).

Now back to our regularly scheduled program . . . "How to Get Babies to Sleep Through the Night." To help Charlotte, we always stick to a consistent, peaceful, and calming bedtime ritual—dim the lights, put on soft guitar lullaby music, change her diaper, put on PJs, cuddle in the rocking chair while reading a short book, nurse, hold her and walk up and down the dark hallway, say prayers next to her crib, then kiss good night and lay her down. We take sort of the opposite of the Ferber approach. Charlotte actually slept in our bed the first 3 months, then in a bassinet next to me for another 2, then a crib. On the nights when she cries, I go to her and hold and reassure her, nursing her if she's hungry. I subscribe to the theory that if Charlotte feels totally loved and comforted, she will become more secure, and ultimately less dependent on us. Not sure if that makes sense. . . . My point is that there are a million different "get your baby to sleep" techniques—you need to find the one that feels right to you. Be patient, Darren's still tiny. He'll start sleeping better before you know it.

Cate

P.S. I liked the books *The Baby Book* (Sears & Sears) and *Sweet Dreams* (Fleiss). And I have a friend who swears by *The No-Cry Sleep Solution* (Pantley).

Tuesday, July 3

That's quite a routine, Cate! I wish someone would do all of that for me (all but the diaper).

Anne

Tuesday, July 3

Geez, it's so confusing. Some people tell you that you're spoiling your baby by picking him up every time he cries, and other people tell you that it's impossible to spoil a baby. It's like listening to politicians saying opposite things with equal conviction, and both are convincing. Like Cate, we set a consistent and predictable routine, but not only at night— all throughout the day. Nurse, sleep, play, nurse, sleep, play . . . I'm sure this helped, but I think we were also just plain lucky with Caleb. When he was 7 weeks, we took him up to the mountains for the weekend. That first night, he slept for 6 hours. I woke up after 5 hours in a panic and rushed over to the Pack and Play—there he was sleeping like an angel. Maybe it was the altitude? From that night on, he slept through the night. So maybe you need to plan a long weekend getaway in the mountains!

Andrea

SLEEPLESS IN SEATTLE, DENVER, DES MOINES, NEW YORK . . .

Remember the friends, neighbors, relatives, and strangers who told you while you were pregnant that you should try to savor your last nights of uninterrupted sleep? Maybe you shrugged off their comments, thinking, *I've been tired before—what's the big deal?* After all, you're already up six times a night to pee and you're surviving. Or maybe you took your friends' comments seriously but thought sleep deprivation wouldn't affect you like it affected them. You made plans to "sleep while your baby sleeps" and read articles about how to get a good power nap.

But after having a baby, you discovered that there's tired . . . and then there's *tired*. Your body just performed the most demanding task Mother Nature will ask of it, and now there's no time to relax, rest, and recover. As a result, the exhaustion you experience the first few weeks after having a baby can feel dizzying and endless, as though someone has tampered with your equilibrium and you're living in a parallel universe. You've got a new baby to tend to around the clock, and no matter what you do, you can't seem to get the rest you so badly need. You feel as if you're pulling all-nighters every night and desperately await the night you'll get to sleep for more than two hours in succession. Then, as you begin to hit your stride as a new mom and feel that you're learning to cope with being tired, the end of your maternity leave looms. You start to wonder how you will be able to add work back into the mix, especially if your baby isn't sleeping through the night yet.

Just as you can't know when your baby will first roll over

or smile, there's no way to predict when she will sleep through the night. There's no "right age" when your baby should sleep through the night, though many experts agree that by the time a baby is six months she is capable of doing so. And by the way, when you hear about a baby sleeping through the night at five weeks, this usually means that she slept for five or six hours without a feeding. Now is the time to give up the notion that when your baby sleeps through the night you'll be getting eight or nine hours of sleep again. You won't—instead, you'll create a new definition of what a good night's sleep is. In fact, sleeping for five or six hours straight will seem downright divine.

Thursday, July 5

I was complaining to my dad about lack of sleep and he told me that sleep deprivation is actually a form of torture. I Googled it and brought this article in for us. Check the part I highlighted—*symptoms include disorientation, losing the ability to act and think coherently, intense stress accompanied by a wearying haze.* Sound familiar?

Cate

P.S. I brought Milk Duds for everyone! How appropriate, coming from me.

Thursday, July 5

So it's real—we're not crazy after all! Or maybe we are crazy, but at least we know why!

MOO, Stacy (Yummy Milk Duds.)

COPING AT WORK WHEN
YOU'RE A ZOMBIE

This much we know: When you return to work, you're going to be tired. On top of the basic difficulty of going back to work, you'll be stressed about doing your work well when you're in a sleepy fog. Our advice is to take a deep breath and remain calm. Be patient—with yourself and your baby. Hopefully your coworkers will understand that your transition back to work is not like flipping a switch. With an infant at home, you can't instantly regain your stride at work. There will be days when you're "on," and days when you'd like to bring a pillow to work along with your briefcase and breastpump. We know of one Milk Mama who dozed off during a staff meeting (which are snoozers even for the well rested), and others who took occasional catnaps in their cars during lunchtime. These women are still gainfully employed, and you will be too. Try not to worry about the dark circles, frequent yawns, and slow-firing brain synapses. This, too, shall pass. In the meantime, try these coping strategies.

- *Go outside*. Get some fresh air and get your blood pumping. Can't go outside? Stand up and stretch. Breathe deeply; take in oxygen.
- *Don't focus on how many times your were up at night or at what time*. Checking the clock each time you are awake makes you dwell on your misery, constantly reminding yourself and anyone who will listen, "Last night I was up at eleven, one-fifteen, three-thirty, and five for thirty minutes each time!!"
- *Savor a cup of coffee when you need it*. You don't have to avoid caffeine completely. A very small amount makes its way into breastmilk, and most babies are not affected by your drinking one or two cups of coffee per day.
- *Structure your workday in chunks*. Vary the activities so you're stimulated. Also, if you're a morning person, do the hardest tasks first (or vice versa) when you're the most alert.
- *Give yourself a break*. Don't take on too many chores and errands after work. Some Mamas find it more manageable to do grocery shopping, cleaning, and laundry in small chunks each day; others prefer to set aside Sunday morn-

ing to crank it all out. Whatever you decide, temporarily lower your standards for cleanliness and a well-stocked refrigerator. Enjoy some quiet time with your little one, and relax.

- *Plan low-key weekends.* Take advantage of naps (turn off the phone) if you have someone (husband, neighbor, friend) who can help. Don't plan more than one major outing a day.

- *Reserve a night when you will get uninterrupted sleep.* This could mean going to the basement or guest bedroom or checking into a hotel! Ask your husband, partner, relative, or friend to be "on duty" that night.

- *Put things into perspective.* When all else fails and your body aches for sleep, remind yourself that the reason you are so exhausted is because you have been blessed with an amazing, beautiful baby.

Thursday, July 5

I've eaten so many of these Milk Duds that I think my breastmilk is going to come out chocolate!

Steph

Thursday, July 5

Chocolate breastmilk—oh no! What's that going to do to our already wired babies?

Disoriented, incoherent, stressed, and hazy,

Anne

Thursday, July 5

Crazy as it sounds, part of me would be happy if Charlotte were wired in the evenings. I hate not being with her in the mornings when she's most alert, and I find myself hoping she won't fall asleep too early in the evening. I work so hard at trying to get her to sleep and then feel upset if she falls asleep before I've had my fill of her! As working moms, will we ever get enough time with them?

Cate

HELPING YOUR BABY SLEEP THROUGH THE NIGHT

Philosophies for getting babies to sleep through the night are as different as breastmilk and Diet Coke, only it's less obvious which one is right for your baby. At the bookstore or library, you can find entire shelves of baby sleep books.

One book tells you to let your baby cry, while the one right next to it adamantly argues that you should never leave him to cry it out. As more moms return to the workforce, books on the topic have become best-sellers. That's because dealing with so-called baby sleep "problems" is a real dilemma for working moms. On the one hand, we desperately need our sleep in order to be functional at work, but on the other hand, we long to soothe and connect with our babies at night since we're away from them during the day!

This desire for connection time may spur you to continue nighttime feedings despite your need for more sleep. Nursing your baby in the silent darkness while holding her close as you rub her hair and listen to her swallow and breathe can be surprisingly peaceful. Furthermore, breastfeeding through the night keeps your supply up and is nurturing for your little one. Over time, your baby will begin to associate breastfeeding with comfort, security, warmth, and closeness. These emotional needs are every bit as important as her needs for nourishment. Your baby was designed to wake up during the night to eat and cuddle. What society sees as a sleep problem is often just your baby's natural instinct, and responding to these needs can enhance her sense of security and well-being. That said, you must pay attention to your own sleep requirements, because what your baby ultimately needs is a happy, well-rested mom.

How Much Babies Typically Sleep
Approximate—Actual Results May Vary!

	SLEEP DURATION		DAYTIME NAPS		
Age of Baby	Total per day	Longest Single Period	Qty.	Total Nap Duration	When Naps Occur
1 week	16 to 17 hours	2 to 5 hours	5 to 7	Varies	Anyone's Guess
6 to 8 weeks	15 to 16 hours	4 to 9 hours	3 to 5	Varies	Anyone's Guess
3 to 4 months	15 to 16 hours	7 to 9 hours	2 to 3	3 to 5 hours	Mid-morning Early Afternoon, (Possibly) Early Evening
4 to 8 months	14 to 16 hours	7 to 12 hours	2	2.5 to 4 hours	Mid-morning, Early Afternoon
9 to 12 months	14 to 15 hours	10 to 12 hours	1 to 2	2.5 to 3.5 hours	(Recommended) Mid-morning, Early Afternoon
12 to 18 months	14 hours	10 to 12 hours	1 to 2	2 to 3 hours	(Possibly) Mid-morning, Early Afternoon

Sources: *Healthy Sleep Habits, Happy Child* by Marc Weissbluth, M.D., and *Solve Your Child's Sleep Problems* by Richard Ferber, M.D., American Academy of Pediatrics

Sleep Baby, Sleep!
(Progression of Sleep Development)

CHILD'S AGE	NEW SLEEP DEVELOPMENT
6 weeks	Night sleep lengthens
12 to 16 weeks	Daytime sleep becomes more regular, night sleep cycles become more adult-like
9 months	Daytime naps lengthen, night wakings for feeding are no longer needed, most babies take 2 (rather than 3) naps
12 to 21 months	Most children take 1 early afternoon nap (morning nap disappears)
3 to 4 years	Afternoon nap becomes less common

Source: *Healthy Sleep Habits, Happy Child* by Marc Weissbluth, M.D.

THREE IN THE BED

If you're not ready to give up nighttime feedings but are desperate for more sleep, one option is to share your bed with your baby. Some parents find that everyone sleeps better when in the same bed, but this practice, known as cosleeping, is controversial in the United States. The U.S. Product Consumer Safety Commission (CPSC) warns against placing infants in adult beds. They say it puts babies at risk of suffocation (from an adult rolling on top of the baby or from the baby getting trapped between the mattress and the headboard or bed and wall) and strangulation (babies getting their heads stuck in a headboard opening). According to the CPSC, during a seven-year period (1990 to 1997), 515 children under the age of two died after being put to sleep on an adult bed. Supporters, however, argue that infants who sleep in a safe adult bed with a safe (sober, nonsmoking) adult have a lower death risk than those sleeping in a crib in another room. They also argue that cosleeping makes breast-feeding more convenient, helps moms synchronize their sleeping cycles with their babies', helps babies fall asleep, and allows working moms to regain intimacy with their babies that they missed during the day.

Indeed, cosleeping can be a very attractive option for working moms. Instead of waking up and getting out of bed to nurse your (crying, fully awake) baby several times throughout the night, you can wake just enough to snuggle up to your (half-asleep) baby and nurse her. From your baby's perspective, this arrangement keeps her near you when she needs you most and helps her feel comforted and less alone.

If you decide to give cosleeping a try, take safety precautions. Although you've no doubt heard plenty of warnings about the danger of rolling on top of your baby, the truth is that moms all over the world cosleep without smothering their babies. Most moms will tell you that even while they sleep, they remain aware of their babies' presence next to them. To set up a safe sleeping environment, make sure your mattress fits tightly in the bed frame (no waterbeds), and that your headboard doesn't have any openings that could trap your baby's head. Place your baby on her back between you and your husband/partner and away from pillows (and other fluffy or heavy bedding), so there isn't any danger of your baby falling off the bed or suffocating. You might want to try a small bassinet made for cosleeping in your bed, or a product (round fabric-covered frame or wedge) that helps keep your baby from rolling over. If you want to sleep next to your husband *and* your baby, you could place your baby in a cosleeping bassinet that attaches to the side of your bed. Keep pets or older children out of the bed, and of course, don't cosleep (or breastfeed!) if you are drunk, high, or heavily medicated.

As you consider cosleeping, you might find yourself wondering whether or not you'll ever have sex with your husband again. Let's face it, in the early months after having a baby, sex isn't exactly what it once was anyway. And for rare romantic occasions, you can always find a place other than your bed to have some "private time." As your child grows, he will eventually wean himself of your bed on his own, but if waking up to a wiggly two-year-old isn't what you envisioned when you started cosleeping, you can transition him to the crib as soon as you are ready. Making this move by the time your baby is six months is easiest, before his habit of sleeping with you is ingrained.

Like many of the decisions you will make during your child's lifetime, there's no right or wrong answer when it comes to cosleeping. You have to choose the method that you're comfortable with and that works best for your family.

MAKING A CHANGE

Once you're ready to reduce nighttime feedings and change your baby's sleeping habits, finding the right solution is a matter of determining what fits best with your parenting style. Whether you gravitate toward a more disciplined, scheduled approach or toward a looser, more free-flowing one, here are ten tips. As with all parenting advice, pick the pearls that work for you, and leave the rest.

1. *Stick to a consistent bedtime.* Don't wait until your baby is overtired, cranky, rubbing her eyes, or yawning before putting her to bed. If you notice your baby winding down at 7:30 P.M., make that her bedtime. By sticking to a specific bedtime night after night (weekends included), you will help your baby set her internal sleep clock.

2. *Don't cave.* A corollary to sticking to a consistent bedtime is not caving in. As a working mom, it can be very

tempting to keep your baby up late so you can spend quality time with her after you've been away all day. But skimping on your baby's sleep is not a good idea. Sleep not only gives your child time to process and store information but it triggers the release of a human growth hormone, which is necessary for physical development. Sleep is also essential to building the immune system and helping your baby fight infection.

3. *Establish a calming bedtime routine.* About thirty minutes before bedtime, start a nighttime ritual, which could include dimming the lights, nursing, singing a song, reading a book, or giving a bath or massage. At the end of the routine, put your baby in his crib whether he is asleep or awake. Your baby will begin to associate this routine with falling asleep. Also, when a babysitter or nanny puts your baby to bed, make sure they know and follow the same routine as you. Some people may tell you not to nurse or rock your baby to sleep because then she could have a hard time falling asleep on her own. Keep in mind that a baby's desire to nurse to sleep is normal. Just as adults read or watch TV before bed to get ready for sleep, babies use nursing as the ultimate way to relax. And what a beautiful, memorable moment for you. There is nothing sweeter or more harmonious than watching your baby fall

asleep at your breast. Learning to fall asleep without nursing is a developmental milestone that your baby will naturally reach when she is ready.

4. *Swaddle your baby.* For the first three months, your baby should be swaddled in a blanket at bedtime. Infants who are swaddled wake up less often and sleep longer because their own sudden movements are less likely to disturb them if their arms and legs are contained.

5. *Put your baby to bed awake.* If you prefer not to nurse or rock your baby to sleep, try putting her to bed awake. Some experts believe this teaches your baby to fall asleep on her own when she awakens throughout the night (all babies wake up two to six times per night).

6. *Let the sun shine.* Expose your baby to about thirty minutes of light every morning. Light suppresses the release of the sleep hormone melatonin. In turn, this helps set your baby's internal clock and makes it easier for her to sleep at night.

7. *Don't skip naps.* Set a regular napping schedule for your baby. While it may seem logical to keep your baby up all day so she will be more tired at night, this plan almost always backfires. When babies sleep during the day, they are more relaxed, calmer, and easier to put to bed at night. They also tend to sleep better through the night; children who are sleep deprived wake up more often at night.

8. *Wait and see.* It's normal for babies to wake up or cry out as they move from one sleep cycle to the next. Often, they can go right back to sleep without your help. So try not to rush to your baby's side every time you hear a peep.

9. *Don't start solids too early.* You've probably heard that giving your baby cereal will help him sleep longer during the night, but this isn't true. A baby's digestive system isn't ready for solids until sometime around six months, and solids given too early can actually upset a baby's tummy and cause your baby to develop food allergies. In addition, feeding your baby solids too early could decrease your milk supply. Formula-fed babies, on the other hand, do tend to go longer between feedings because formula is harder to digest than breastmilk. Although switching to formula may sound like an appealing solution, you already know that breastmilk is the best food on earth. If you can stick with breastmilk, that's the way to go.

10. *Take heart.* Every child eventually learns to sleep through the night. Sleep deprivation won't last forever. Believe it or not, a year from now, you may fondly look back on the first few months when your baby was so tiny and utterly dependent on you.

MAMA KNOWS BEST

Whichever method you choose to help your baby sleep through the night, keep in mind that the approach that works for one baby might not work for the next. Also, be sure to evaluate your motives for changing your baby's sleep habits in the first place. Ask yourself if your baby seems happy and well rested. Then, ask yourself if *you* are happy and well rested (well, maybe just ask yourself if you are happy). Over time, if your baby's sleep patterns are affecting your job, marriage, or relationship with your other children, or if you feel angry or resentful, it's time for a change. But if you're changing your baby's sleep patterns because Great-grandma Dorothy says you're not doing things the way she did them back in the day, slow down. If you're enjoying nighttime feedings, continue them. If you want to give cosleeping a try, take the necessary safety precautions and go for it. Your goal is to get the right amount of sleep while still respecting the needs of your baby. When you change under pressure from others you won't be as committed, and you'll be changing for the wrong reasons. Helping your baby to sleep through the night works best if you are motivated, consistent, and able to choose the approach and timing that works for everyone in your family.

EIGHT

· · ·

stressed breast

Ladies,

It feels like there's a fun-size Snickers bar in my left breast! It's killing me! This used to happen when I was nursing Colby, but back then it was more of a Tootsie Roll. I think it's all Ferber's fault! George is already starting to sleep better through the night, which means he's nursing less. Plus, for some reason he drank less than usual this morning. So now he's probably starving while I'm here in pain. Ouch!!

Stacy

P.S. You guys know I'm talking about a plugged duct, right?

Monday, July 9

I'm glad you clarified, because I thought you were talking about stashing candy in your bra, which would get pretty messy! I've never had a plugged duct, so I'm not much help. Is this one more thing for me to worry about?

Andrea

Monday, July 9

Stacy,

Hope your plugged duct gets better!!

You'll all be glad to know that I dropped Ryan and Ella off today at the new day care, and it went great.

Hooray!

Anne

Monday, July 9

Anne,

WOO HOO!

Stacy,

Oh, I hate plugged ducts! My Milk Dud gets plugged a lot. The few sprinklers it has are defective. Have you tried the warm wet washcloth technique?

Cate

Monday, July 9

Yep, I've already tried the WWWT. Not working—probably because I'm using paper towels and a pump instead of a washcloth and a baby. I think I'll go home early.

Stacy

Monday, July 9

Clue me in to the WWWT— I might need to use it someday! Stacy, I hope by the time you're reading this tomorrow, the Snickers bar is gone.

Andrea

Tuesday, July 10

Better, Stacy?

Anne

Tuesday, July 10

Yes! Got through the plugged duct. Thank God.

Andrea, if you ever get one, here's the trick. You stand over a sink and hold a washcloth (as warm as you can stand it) against your breast for a few minutes. Then you immediately nurse your baby while massaging the lump/Snicker's bar. Plugs can be caused by making too much milk (see, there *are* some downsides to being a dairy cow) or not fully draining your breast. Plugs can then lead to mastitis—I'm an expert on that too! Plugs, infections, bites, cracked nipples, milk blisters—you name it, my breasts have had it and conquered it.

Bring it on,

Stacy

Tuesday, July 10

OMG! If I have to go through any of that, it will push me over the edge to formula land. Your dedication is amazing.

Steph

Tuesday, July 10

What? Milk blisters? This is the stuff they don't tell you in childbirth class. Luckily, I haven't really had a painful breastfeeding experience (knock on this medical table). Besides engorgement, trying to protect my nipples from the searing pain of water hitting them in the shower (during the early nursing days), and a few uncomfortable pumping sessions with P.I.S., I think my breasts have done pretty well. I'm totally impressed that you've been through it all and are still nursing.

You go girl, Andrea

P.S. Don't you hate the word *engorgement*?

A LIFE OF THEIR OWN

Remember the days when you just put your breasts in a bra and forgot about them? As a nursing mom, those days are long gone and your breasts have now taken on a life of their own. They're full, they're empty, they're hard, they're soft, they're in a pump, in your baby's mouth, squirting milk, leaking milk—making you constantly aware of them. Not surprisingly, all of this activity can sometimes lead your breasts to revolt. Every breastfeeding book has lengthy sections devoted to breast problems: plugged ducts, milk blisters, thrush, mastitis, abscesses, engorgement, and cracked, sore, and bleeding nipples. What's worse, when you look at what's been written you see words like "shooting, burning, searing, exquisite, stabbing" to describe the pain associated with these conditions. It's not a rosy picture. As a new mom, you not only have to take care of your new baby, you also have to take care of his life source: your breasts. While it's unlikely you will experience most of these problems, it's a good idea for you and your breasts to be informed and ready, just in case.

🍼 *milk mama tip*

If you experience any of the breast problems described in this chapter, call a certified lactation consultant for help.

CALL THE PLUMBER

Probably the most common ailment is plugged milk ducts. These occur when a clog in one of the milk ducts stops milk from flowing. The milk gets backed up, causing a tender, lumpy, and sometimes reddish area that doesn't improve with nursing or pumping. Some moms see a white pimple-like bump right on the nipple, which is a milk blister, or plugged nipple pore. Plugged ducts and nipple pores result from a lack of milk movement, often caused by a change in your baby's feeding routine. Just when you think you've reached easy street because your baby is sleeping through the night, you wake up with a plugged duct! Plugs can also result from incomplete or uneven emptying of the breast, infrequent nursing, separation from baby, and fatigue. Let's see . . . Are you tired? Are you separated from your baby for hours at a time? Is your pump less efficient than your baby when it comes to draining your breastmilk? No wonder working moms are particularly susceptible to plugged ducts!

Take a few preventive steps from the start to avoid plugged ducts: get plenty of rest (heard this before?), drink lots of water (sound familiar?), pump at least two or three times a day using a high-quality, efficient pump, and nurse frequently when you're with your baby (ditto, ditto). The same measures that will keep your supply up will help prevent plugged ducts. Also, you should wear loose-fitting, comfortable bras and avoid baby carriers with tight straps. When you nurse, vary positions so that your baby has a chance to reach and drain all the milk ducts (a baby's position on the breast draws milk from some ducts more than others). When you pump, don't rush—allow time to completely drain your breasts.

If you do experience a plugged duct, you should treat it immediately so it doesn't become infected. Start by applying a warm, moist compress for fifteen to twenty minutes right before you nurse or pump (the Warm Wet Washcloth Technique). This won't be easy to do while you're at work, but fortunately, plugged ducts usually only last a day or two. Besides, a few long pumping sessions are better than taking days off from work if your plugged duct turns into mastitis. When at home, take a nice, long hot shower or bath and massage your breast. Also, when you're nursing or pumping, massage the tender area of your breast. You can also let gravity help: get on your hands and knees and lean over your baby to nurse him (or hunch over while you pump). It's not exactly the most comfortable position, but it can help a plugged duct open more easily. You'll know when the plug releases because your milk may go shooting across the room, your baby may start gulping, and you'll definitely feel the painful pressure release. Ahhhh.

READ THIS WHILE SITTING DOWN

If you're not better within a week, go to your doctor. Plugged ducts can lead to mastitis, a bacterial infection of the breast. Mastitis can also be caused by an untreated cracked nipple. Symptoms of mastitis are flulike—fever, chills, weakness, and achiness, typically accompanied by soreness and a reddened area on the breast. Treatment for mastitis is the same as for plugged ducts, plus your doctor will probably prescribe antibiotics. Don't worry, there are antibiotics that are safe to take while breastfeeding. Unfortunately, once you take antibiotics, you'll have to watch out for yeast growth (which can result in thrush) and diaper rash. If you get thrush, your nipples may be itchy, shiny, reddened, and tender. Your baby will likely have white "milky" patches inside his cheeks and on his tongue. Because thrush is passed back and forth between mom and baby, both of you will be treated, which involves rubbing nystatin ointment on your nipples, and giving your baby nystatin suspension liquid with a medicine dropper, then swabbing his mouth. Unfortunately, yeast is very hearty and doesn't always disappear with nystatin. In this case, work with a doctor or certified lactation consultant who will recommend a different medicine, a strict hygiene regimen or dietary changes. Nobody said this was going to be easy—or did they?

Not to scare you more, but if mastitis isn't resolved within a few days, you could develop a breast abscess. Although very rare, an abscess is when pus (yuck!) accumulates within the infected part of the breast. Yikes—your breast turns into one big, unpoppable pimple! A physician can drain the abscess surgically or through a series of needle aspirations. The moral of the story is this: As we said, your breasts have taken on a life of their own. Be nice to them. Don't neglect them. Massage them and tell them how wonderful they are.

Wednesday, July 11

I couldn't sleep at all last night, worrying about the things that could go wrong with my breasts! I looked up plugged ducts and mastitis online and I'm happy to report a simple remedy. One doctor recommended exposing your breasts to fresh air and sun! Since IBM has gone so far as to provide this room, do you think they'd designate a lactation court-yard where we could freely sun our naked breasts?

Andrea

Wednesday, July 11

Fresh air and sun? What's that?

Anne

Wednesday, July 11

Our poor breasts! It's bad enough that we have to work in windowless caves all day, but at least *we* get to see the sun as we walk to our cars in the parking lot. They live in bras all day, working hard, making milk, and we only take them out twice a day under these fluorescent lights, stuff them in plas-tic suction cups, and suck them dry. They deserve better!

Cate

Wednesday, July 11

Not only would the lactation courtyard benefit our breasts but imagine the thrill we'd give the engineers around here! On second thought . . . ewwwwww!

Stacy

CRACKED UP

Another fairly common problem is sore, cracked, or bleeding nipples (just thinking about it is enough to give you the heebie-jeebies!). The primary cause is improper positioning of your baby at the breast, but cracks can also be caused by eczema, severe dry skin, or not using your breast pump correctly. If improper positioning is the cause, you'll experience a world of improvement by changing your nursing technique. While nursing, your baby should be tummy-to-tummy and should open wide to get a mouthful of both your nipple and areola. An off-centered latch-on is the best position, where more of the areola below the nipple is in your baby's mouth. When using your pump, make sure the shield is centered on your breast and that the suction strength and cycle rate are comfortable. Of course, while your nipples are recovering, you'll still have to endure the pain of pumping or nursing. This is where the breathing techniques you learned in childbirth class come in handy (just hee-hee-hoooo your pain away). When you're with your baby, you can make things a little more bearable by nursing more frequently, but for a shorter duration. This way, your baby won't suck quite as hard because he's been snacking throughout the day. Rub breastmilk on your nipples after each feeding and let them air dry—the breastmilk contains antibodies that will actually help you heal. Don't use any soap, lotions, or perfumes on your nipples (who perfumes their nipples anyway?). Moist wound healing speeds recovery. Try rubbing lanolin ointment or using a breast gel pack on your nipples, which allows the wound to heal without forming a scab. Be glad you weren't breastfeeding in the '80s when, believe it or not, drying your nipples with a hair dryer or sun lamp was in vogue.

Wednesday, July 11

Sorry to do this to you, Andrea, but here's another thing for you to worry about. You know how pierced nipples are all the rage? Well, I guess I was ahead of the trend because when Colby was a baby, he pierced my nipples with his teeth! As soon as babies get teeth, they chew on everything like a puppy (and their teeth are just as sharp). The first time Colby bit me, I screamed and practically dropped him on the floor . . . he was hanging on for dear life with his teeth. I put that to an end by buying him a shock collar. (Kidding!)

Stacy

Wednesday, July 11

The things we (and our breasts) go through! Instead of a shock collar, Charlotte needs baby dentures. She is still all gums! Will she ever be able to eat anything crunchier than soggy Cheerios?

    Cate

Wednesday, July 11

    At the first sign of teeth, party's over. I'm not as tough as you, Stacy. The thought of biting makes me shiver—or is it this freezing room that gives me the chills?

    Andrea

Thursday, July 12

    Andrea,

    Most babies never bite. You can breastfeed long after Caleb gets teeth. Just you wait—I bet you won't be ready to quit when his pearly whites appear.

    Stacy

Thursday, July 12

    Teeth or no teeth, I don't know if Darren will be getting breastmilk much longer. My goal is five months (mid-August). I'm sorry to say this but I can't wait to be done.

    Steph

Thursday, July 12

Steph,

Don't be sorry for one minute! Be proud of yourself for every day you've pumped to give Darren breastmilk. Your dedication is amazing! And besides, we're all in this together— it's not a competition. We'll help you make it to your goal.

Cate

DON'T BITE THE BREAST
THAT FEEDS YOU

Even if you're able to weather or steer clear of breast ailments and infections, there's one thing that's inevitable—your baby will get teeth. Many moms decide to wean their babies when teeth appear, but the truth is, the majority of breastfed babies never bite their moms. And even if you have a biter, it's an easy problem to nip (ha) in the bud. Teeth sprout at all different ages, but on average, the first tooth breaks through at about six months. Because the first teeth usually appear on your baby's lower gum, it's virtually impossible for her to bite because her tongue covers her teeth while she's breastfeeding. However, as more teeth appear, your baby might try to take a bite, and the sharp surprise will no doubt get your attention.

Your reaction ("Ouch!") may startle your baby so that she

doesn't do it again. It's more common, however, for her to be curious enough to see if it works again. If this happens, stay calm but stop feeding her, make eye contact, and firmly say, "No biting." Most babies don't like abrupt interruptions while nursing, and this technique helps them associate biting with being taken off the breast. The trick is breaking the latch properly (gently putting your finger in the corner of her mouth to break the seal), rather than instinctively yanking her off your nipple. Also, if you see that your baby is about to bite, you can insert your finger so that she bites that instead of your breast, and follow up by firmly telling her "No biting." Whatever you do, *do not* try to pull your baby from your breast while her jaws are clamped down—unless you want to feel shooting, burning, searing, exquisite, stabbing pain all at once!

If biting persists, you can try reinforcing the "No biting" message by putting your baby down for a few minutes after she bites. If that doesn't work, don't give up. There are many reasons a baby bites: pain due to teething, frustration that letdown isn't happening quickly enough, thrush, mouth ulcers, because she wants to be playful, is distracted, or wants attention. If you think the cause of biting is teething and sore gums, you can try to satisfy your baby's need to bite by giving her a cold teething ring before or after you nurse. If you think your baby is trying to get your attention by biting, be sure to give her your total, undivided attention while nursing. Also, give your baby lots of praise, hugs, and kisses when she doesn't bite.

Average Ages for Infant Teething

AGE	TEETH	POSITION
6 to 7 months	Incisors	Two central bottom and two central top teeth
7 to 9 months	Two more incisors	Top and bottom, making four top and four bottom teeth in all
10 to 14 months	First molars	Double teeth for chewing
15 to 18 months	Canines	The pointed teeth or "fangs"
2 to 3 years	Second molars	The second set of double teeth at the back

Source: www.thenewparentsguide.com

Friday, July 13

My breasts are stressed just thinking about your battle scars, Stacy! On a happy note, Ryan started giggling! Is there any better sound in the whole world?

Anne

P.S. I brought in some real fun-size Snickers bars. Indulge!

• • •

bottle strike

PANIC. Ryan WILL NOT take a bottle! What is going on with him?! He's been taking a bottle like a champ since he was 3 weeks old. Last Thursday the new day-care lady said he wouldn't eat at all. Totally refused. I thought maybe Ryan was just upset about being in a new place, or maybe my breastmilk had gone bad, so I raced there and nursed him. The next day, same thing. I think the milk is actually fine— he just suddenly hates the bottle. Out of the blue. I can't believe this is happening to me. I'm already stressed out with work, a baby, a 4-year-old, and no husband (or boyfriend, for that matter) to lean on. I can't keep leaving work. But I can't stand the thought of Ryan (10th percentile featherweight) starving all day. Have your babies ever refused the bottle?

Anne

Monday, July 16

Anne,

What a nightmare. Charlotte went on a bottle strike at about the same age—3 months. I also introduced the bottle around 3 weeks, knowing I would be returning to work. One day, it was as if I was trying to feed her battery acid. She freaked out if the bottle got anywhere near her, and for a brief moment, I thought that would be my get-out-of-work ticket . . . but then I remembered the mortgage.

I tried everything. Had my husband feed her the bottle instead of me (since she knows I have the goods on me). Nope. Tried every bottle-nipple combo on the market. Nope. Called my lactation consultant bawling. She didn't have a quick fix, but suggested a lot of love and patience. It sounds crazy, but it's the one thing that worked. Ask your caregiver to hold Ryan calmly and lovingly when he cries, to let Ryan know she understands that he's mad and he wants mommy, but mommy's not available right now. Tell her not to force the bottle, but to back off, comfort him, and offer it again gently every half hour or so throughout the day. Give it a couple days—it took Charlotte about four—and Ryan will take the bottle again. Have faith.

Cate

Monday, July 16

Anne,

your little Ryan prefers to drink straight from the tap!
(Can we blame him?) Poor little thing. Only have a couple
minutes, but maybe you could ask the day-care lady to put a
drop of breastmilk on the bottle nipple to make it more appealing. Or have her feed Ryan in a different setting—
outside, bouncy seat, etc. Or would it be possible for your
neighbor to bring Ryan here to IBM for you to nurse him?
Another thought: sometimes babies just decide to fast during the day and nurse like crazy all night. If Ryan seems to
be eating more at night, maybe he's just adjusting his eating
schedule to nurse when he can be with you.

Hug, Stacy

Tuesday, July 17

Well, I guess that's one thing I have going for me, being
a pumper and bottle feeder from day 1. Gerber nipples are
the only ones Darren knows. Hang in there, Anne.

Steph

Tuesday, July 17

Thank you so much for understanding, caring, and offering
tips. The thing is my new day-care lady watches 3 other kids
besides Ryan and Ella, and one of them is 3 months old, same

as Ryan . . . so she can't exactly hold Ryan all day, never mind loading them all up in the car so Ryan can nurse here at IBM. I'll ask (beg, plead with) her to try some of the other ideas. THANKS! Stacy, I haven't noticed him eating more at night— but then again, for the last week I've been trying to get him to take a bottle in the evening. I'll try nursing him more often.

(Raggedy) Anne

Wednesday, July 18

My second week back, Caleb (also a featherweight) cried his head off and refused his bottle. My aunt called me but all I could hear was Caleb crying in the background. I totally blew off a meeting and raced to her house to nurse him. When I picked him up and rubbed his back, he let out a big fraternity-boy burp, and that was the end of that. Turns out he wasn't on a bottle strike after all. Anne, I wish it could be that simple for you!

Big Hug, Andrea

P.S. Let's hear it for Caleb, who is now 6 months and has had no formula! Think I can actually breastfeed for a whole year?

Wednesday, July 18

I'm a wreck. Nothing is working and my day-care provider is no help. I think she's doing the best she can, but she keeps mentioning that Ryan is not in danger of starving. I think she's trying to reassure me. *Of course* I know he won't starve, but more than the hunger I worry about the fact that he's completely *miserable*, yet he can't express it other than crying all day. I just know he misses me and it kills me.

Anne

A bottle strike is difficult for any mom to weather, but when you work outside the home it is a nightmare. It's hard enough to leave your baby, but the stress is compounded when your baby won't eat because he clearly wants *you*. Many mothers think they have it made when their babies take the bottle happily at three or four weeks old. But it's fairly common for babies to go through a bottle strike of some degree around three months of age. For newborn babies, sucking is a reflex, making bottle introduction fairly easy. By three months, babies begin to outgrow feeding by reflex and begin feeding by choice. They can now "choose to refuse" the silicone nipple in favor of mom's warm breast and cozy embrace. What's a working mom to do? Even the most flexible work situations cannot accommodate mom taking off three or four times a day, especially if there's a commute involved.

BOTTLE BLUNDERS

Don't quit just yet (breastfeeding or working). There is a solution. You and your baby can get through this, but be sure to avoid some common mistakes. For starters, don't listen to anyone who says, "Don't worry. When your baby gets hungry enough, he'll eat." Please. Hunger is not the issue. No one should starve a baby into submission, or engage in a bottle battle, repeatedly jamming the nipple into baby's screaming mouth. If you or your caregiver try three times and your baby refuses, give it a rest. If you're there, don't nurse her right away. Wait fifteen minutes so that you're not *immediately* rewarding her strike. Don't blame yourself for not successfully teaching her to drink from a bottle. Don't feel guilty about needing to give her a bottle so that you can return to work. Remember and cherish all the time you do spend with her, and pat yourself on the back for breastfeeding in the first place!

THERE IS HOPE

Friday, July 20

Progress! My day-care lady just called to report that she tried giving Ryan a bottle while holding him on her porch swing—and he took it!! Go figure. I don't want to get my hopes up. I'm wondering if he will refuse again on Monday after being with me all weekend. Maybe I should try giving him a bottle or two over the weekend so he doesn't get spoiled.

Anne

P.S. Ryan is so cute. He likes to be on the floor all day long kicking and straightening his little legs. With all his leg lifts, he's going to have abs of steel!

Friday, July 20

Anne,

I'm so glad to hear Ryan took a bottle. I think it's a good idea to offer him bottles this weekend—though it seems sad to think that breastfeeding could ever "spoil" a baby. That is *mixed up*! But I guess it's something we working moms have to cope with. Hang in there.

Cate

Monday, July 23

Weekend bottle experiment results: Anne—0; Ella—2. My 4-year-old daughter apparently has the touch. She held the bottle for Ryan while he sat in his bouncy seat. I was silently jumping for joy in the next room. Ella promised to be a "Big Helper" today at day care. Let's all keep our fingers crossed. ·

Anne

Monday, July 23

CHARLOTTE CAN CRAWL!

Cate

P.S. I tried pumping with my fingers crossed (for you, Anne) but it was too hard to hold on to my bottles.

There are many techniques that can help your baby overcome his sudden distaste for bottles. As with most parenting dilemmas, there is no magic solution. Sometimes it's as simple as a different nipple or a new feeding position or location. Sometimes the baby mysteriously gets over his bottle aversion on his own.

Unfortunately, sometimes it's not that simple. If this is the case, try patient persistence with a heaping dose of love. Ask whoever is giving the bottle to make sure that your baby is happy—not too tired or starving. Have them cuddle your baby close, maintain eye contact, and gently offer the bottle. The important thing is for that person to sympathize with your baby, remain calm, and not to rush the process. Trust us, this may sound like some New Age "I'm Okay, You're Okay" technique, but it really can work. You have the best chance for success if you leave the house. Babies can smell mommy's milk from a distance of at least twenty feet, so if your breasts (and you) are in the next room, he knows! Plus, it's nearly impossible to listen to your baby cry without wanting to rush in there to hold and nurse him.

bottle strike basics

If your baby begins refusing the bottle, ask your care provider to try the following:

- Problem solve—determine if the baby's refusal may be caused by a cold, an ear infection, thrush, gas, teething, or the need to burp; make sure the milk hasn't gone bad. Try a different batch of milk. Your baby may have a sensitivity to something in your diet; the most likely culprit is cow's milk, followed by soy protein and eggs. Contrary to popular belief, spicy foods and broccoli probably won't cause your baby to be fussy or refuse a bottle.
- Experiment with different bottles, nipples (faster flow), and temperatures.
- Put a drop of breastmilk on the bottle nipple.
- Offer something other than a bottle—sippy cup (even babies can learn to use one), spoon, or medicine dropper.

- Don't rush or try to force-feed the bottle. If the baby refuses, put the bottle down and wait five to fifteen minutes before trying again.
- Mimic the cuddling, closeness, and calm of breastfeeding. Make eye contact with the baby and gently offer the bottle.
- Try the bait-and-switch method—start with pacifier, then sneak the bottle nipple in.
- Use distraction—vary where and how you feed the baby. Go outside, walk around, face the baby away from you and let him look out the window.
- Call a certified lactation consultant for help!

STUBBORN ALL DAY,
NURSING ALL NIGHT

If you've tried everything and your baby is still refusing milk from a bottle while you're at work, you may notice your baby is nursing more during the evening, middle of the night, and early morning. Your little genius has figured out "reverse-cycle" feeding all on her own, making up for lost milk during the day by bingeing at night. Take heart. Your baby is paying you a compliment—she is so attached to you that she doesn't want to accept a substitute; she's willing to wait for you. While reverse-cycle feeding means less sleep for you, there are also benefits. You'll worry less about your baby being hungry all day, knowing you can provide breastmilk and cuddles at night. It can mean less pumping while you're at work because you're storing up for the nighttime feast. (Whatever amount you do pump during the day could be added to the frozen stockpile.) Remember that night nursing won't last forever; it keeps your supply up, and you might just learn to relish those quiet, intimate times of reconnecting with your baby.

THIS TOO SHALL PASS

Tuesday, July 24

Official update: Ryan took 1½ bottles yesterday (he's still loving the porch swing and his Big Helper, Ella)! Woo-hoo!

Anne

Tuesday, July 24

I propose a toast. Let us raise our milk bottles to Ryan. May he continue to drink his mother's precious breastmilk out of bottles when her breasts are elsewhere. May he grow big and strong, live long and prosper. And may he always know his mother's love.

Cate

TEN

. . .

crying over spilled milk

Does anybody have an extra pair of pants??? I just pumped milk all over mine. I forgot to attach my bottles. What a mess (and a waste of milk). Of course I have a 10:30 meeting. I already took off my pants and tried drying them under the hand dryer, praying the milk stains would disappear (which they didn't) and that no one would walk in (which they didn't). Since having a baby, I've lowered my standards—for modesty and for what's clean enough to wear out of the house. This is a new low. I guess I'll go to the meeting and try to hide my legs under the conference table.

Ready for this day to end,

Andrea

Monday, August 6

Andrea,

Sorry—no spare pants (not to mention the fact that you're a size 4!), but more importantly I'm mourning your spilled breastmilk. Maybe I'm hypersensitive because my nanny just spilled a whole fricking bottle of my milk. She totally doesn't get it. She thinks there's plenty in the freezer (only 22 ounces!) and gave me a "What's the big deal?" look. Am I overreacting? It's not like I can go to the store and buy another gallon of breastmilk.

Cate

Monday, August 6

Ladies,

This stuff is Liquid Gold! You should dock your nanny's pay $100 for every ounce she spills. My caregiver (the one who gave my milk to another baby) is equally clueless. For months, when I picked up George from day care, his bottles were all empty. One day I asked, "Am I giving you enough milk for George? There's never anything left in his bottles at the end of the day." She casually told me that George *never* finished his bottles. She was pouring the leftovers down the drain! She's very by-the-book, and insisted breastmilk wasn't reusable. I tried to remain calm as I told her to please reuse my breastmilk. I can't even think about how many ounces are now in the wastewater treatment center. Grrrrrrr!

Stacy

Monday, August 6

The first time I caught Chad pouring my milk down the drain, I freaked. Even though I have two shelves full of breast-milk in the freezer, it's NOT OK to waste ANY. Especially considering what we have to go through to make the stuff.

Steph

P.S. Check out the new pic I brought of Darren blowing spit bubbles. Nobody but us moms would think spit bubbles are so cute!

Tuesday, August 7

The whole wasted milk thing makes me crazy. I try not to think about how many ounces of my hard-earned milk Caleb has spit right back up. I know it's not the same as spilling (or pouring out!) a bottle of milk, but still, it's a waste of Liquid Gold. I'm going to have a serious talk with Caleb about the importance of breastmilk conservation!

Andrea

P.S. I am certain the expression "crying over spilled milk" was coined by a breastmilk-pumping mom!

P.P.S. Impressive spit bubbles!

MILK MISFORTUNES

Every mom has a tragic story about spilled milk. Be prepared—it's painful to see your baby's next meal in a puddle on the floor or trickling down the drain, especially after you worked so hard to produce it. You know there's more milk brewing, but it's not as if you can just hold a bottle up to the tap and pull the handle.

When you're tired, overwhelmed, and in a rush, it's inevitable that you will occasionally spill milk or accidentally forget to put it in your refrigerator when you get home from work. There's nothing like opening your pump bag the next morning, only to find yesterday's milk still in the compartment, along with the thawed ice packs. Another common mistake is leaving your milk at work. If it's sitting on your desk unrefrigerated, you're faced with driving back to the office to get it, or kissing it good-bye.

Husbands and day-care providers also contribute to milk mishaps. They may thaw three- or four-ounce bags when only an ounce is needed. Or they may spill milk when pouring it from storage bags to bottles. To prevent this, you might suggest they try pouring the milk over a mixing bowl to catch the spillover. One Milk Mama's husband, whose baby was crying hysterically, couldn't wait for the breastmilk to warm up, so he mixed a scoop of emergency backup formula with warm tap water instead. This Mama, who had gone to great lengths to exclusively breastfeed her baby for four months, informed her husband that the formula was only to be used in a true emergency (he's with the baby and the car breaks down and he can't get home), *not* "I can't deal with this screaming child." Also, formula should be prepared using only *cold* tap water to avoid the risk of exposure to lead, which can leach into warm or hot water. One day-care center's contract stipulated that if mothers insisted upon using breastmilk, they would accommodate, but they reserved the right to give the baby formula if the mom didn't provide enough milk.

what you should ask your day-care provider about breastmilk

Some Mamas find it awkward at first to hand a bottle of their own bodily fluid to someone other than a nurse. But with the growing popularity of breastfeeding, day-care providers are typically happy to handle breastmilk and are savvy about storing, warming, and serving it. (See page 119–121 for specific Breastmilk Storage, Thawing, and Warming Guidelines). Just to be sure, you'll want to ask your provider these basic questions:

- Are you familiar with and do you follow the latest milk storage guidelines?
- Do you know how to safely thaw and warm breastmilk?
- Will you refrigerate and reuse any leftover breastmilk? Let her know the reuse parameters you're comfortable with (for example, within two hours versus as long as it doesn't smell bad).
- Will you store a backup supply of my breastmilk in your freezer?
- What will you do if my baby still seems hungry after she has finished her bottles? Let her know if you'd like her to call you at work to see if you're available to nurse your baby.
- Will you check with me before supplementing with formula? Make sure she knows your preferences—whether or not it's OK to use formula, and if so, under what circumstances. Also be clear on how much formula is OK and if she can combine it with your breastmilk.
- Do you require all parents to clearly label milk containers to avoid mix-ups?
- Will you please give my baby X ounces of milk in each bottle? Be specific about your baby's milk intake (and ask her to help you by writing it down—see the Appendix for a sample day-care intake log) so that less (or none!) will be wasted. In general, since breastmilk is digested in less than two hours, it's best to offer a six- to ten-week-old infant small bottles (two to three and a half ounces) frequently.

MILKMARES

Monday, August 13

I had a total *milk*mare last night. I must have still been thinking about my nanny spilling the bottle. In my dream I pumped even more milk than Stacy! I kept having to attach new bottles as the milk gushed out of me—I filled at least 20 bottles and lined them up on this brown table. When I finally finished my pumping session, I stood up and tipped over one of the bottles, then they all fell over like dominoes and the milk went everywhere! That's when I woke up to find that my T-shirt was totally wet with milk. What does THAT mean?

Cate

Monday, August 13

Cate,

That's one crazy dream!

Anne

Tuesday, August 14

Cate,

I think it means that your inner child still craves your mother's love . . . or that you need to let go of your envy of my milk production! Ha.

Stacy

Tuesday, August 14

I've never dreamed about breastmilk, but if I did, I'd dream that Darren had a warm keg of breastmilk at his disposal (à la the keg-erator my college roommate had . . . an old fridge that he modified to have a keg inside and tap outside so we had free-flowing beer at all times). No pumping. No hassle. Infinite supply. That's what dreams are made of!

Steph

Tuesday, August 14

That is so funny! I had a milkmare before I came back to work, when I was crazed with stockpiling milk in the freezer. I dreamed that we had a power outage. My husband, Roger, was all worried about his frozen walleye going bad. Meanwhile I was frantically packing up my frozen milk and calling everyone I knew, but no one had power. I got in my car, turned the air conditioner on full blast and drove 120 mph—

I don't even know where I was going. That's when I woke up, thank God.

Andrea

P.S. What are we going to do if there's a power outage for real???

KEEP IT IN PERSPECTIVE

Over time, you'll probably learn to accept spilled milk as just another inevitable fact of life—like door dings on a new car. There are worse things that can happen. One of our dear Milk Mama friends had to stop breastfeeding sooner than planned because her baby was spitting up constantly, had chronic diarrhea, and wasn't gaining weight. The pediatrician concluded that an *extremely* rare breastmilk allergy was probably the cause. For months our friend couldn't bear to throw out the eighty-plus ounces in her freezer, hoping her baby would miraculously overcome her allergy. Eventually she tearfully discarded the milk and her baby did fine on formula. Compared to our door dings, her car was totaled. Remember this the next time you spill a few ounces, and be grateful for every minute you get to spend snuggling and nursing your little one.

🍼 mothers' milk banks

If you have unused or overly abundant breastmilk, or if your baby has a medical need for more breastmilk than you can provide, a human milk bank may be the answer.

- Milk banks exist to serve: (a) infants with failure to thrive, formula intolerance, allergies, or other medical conditions which require human milk for health or survival, and (b) Mothers with adopted babies, insufficient milk glands, past breast surgery or cancer, medication that contraindicates breastfeeding, or inability to get lactation going to meet their premature babies' needs.

- There are eleven donor milk banks in North America, supervised by the nonprofit Human Milk Banking Association of North America (www.hmbana.org).

- Donor milk recipients need doctors' involvement and prescriptions. Milk can be picked up locally or shipped.

- Donors are meticulously screened for no smoking, no harmful medications, and no communicable diseases. They receive detailed instructions in the hygenic collection and handling of milk.

- Milk banks pasteurize all donated milk to further protect against viruses while retaining most of the nutritional and allergy protection benefits. They also test the milk for bacteria. Milk that is not suitable for infant consumption may still be usable in medical research.

- Milk banks charge recipients a fee to help offset processing costs. Insurance or public assistance may help cover the cost. Donors receive no payment; most of their costs are covered.

Sources: www.breastfeeding.com, Mothers' Milk Bank of Denver Colorado

---

Wednesday, August 15

I have a new question for the expert panel: I discovered 4 ounces of milk in the back of my refrigerator that's 10 days old (drat!). Should I cheat and use it anyway? Or should I throw it out?

Andrea

Wednesday, August 15

Did you smell or taste the milk? If it seems fine to you, use it. If not, for God's sake, don't throw it out. Feed it to the cat. Or if you don't have a cat, give it to a plant!

Stacy

Wednesday, August 15

Andrea,

You could be like my manager and store it in the deep freezer for posterity. She still has a few bags in her freezer and her son just graduated from high school!

Cate

• • •

ELEVEN

breastmilk for the soul

Monday, August 27

Do you guys ever feel like giving up on this whole pumping thing? I do. My workload is killing me, I'm having a hard time sticking to any kind of regular pumping schedule—and when I'm here, I only drip, drip, drip a few ounces. I'm wondering if I should start supplementing with formula or even switch over completely. One part of me feels like pumping is the most meaningful thing I do all day, but another part is so frustrated and tired of it that I'm ready to quit.

Andrea

Monday, August 27

Every day I feel like giving up. Taking time to pump is a giant pain. I have to find someone to answer my phone every time I leave the help desk. And I can't really enjoy nursing

Ryan when I get home because Ella always wants me to do something for her "right now." My goal is 6 months, and I've made it 4½. Where is the fast-forward button?

Anne

Monday, August 27

Committed as I am to exclusive breastfeeding, I'm already counting down the weeks until George turns one! I'm not going to miss pumping at all. Hang in there, Andrea and Anne. Your feelings are normal, and you're doing a great job. Every ounce counts, even if you mix it with formula. Stick with us!

Stacy

Monday, August 27

I hate to disappoint you guys, but I *am* going to give up. I'm proud I made it past 5 months, which I never thought I'd do. Darren will still get breastmilk for another three weeks or so because I have so much stockpiled. Plus, he's eating rice cereal and applesauce now. I'd like to quit cold turkey, but I know the engorgement would be too painful. I'll miss "talking" with you guys and reading about your babies, but this is the pumping session I'll drop first. I'll still drop in to see baby pictures on my way to the cafeteria.

Steph

Monday, August 27

Steph,

Disappointed? No way. We're proud of you and glad we could be your pumping buddies for the final stretch. You know, you could supplement your stockpile with formula (and alternate with breastmilk bottles) to give Darren breastmilk for even longer.

This talk of quitting makes me realize what a kook I am. Not because I love breastfeeding but because I actually like pumping. It's the one thing I do while I'm at work that makes me feel totally connected with Charlotte. It's a chance to unwind and be a *mom*. Plus, it's fun to read the journal. Andrea and Anne, I know it's tough, but we'll cheer you on. Give me an M! Give me an I! Give me an L! Give me a K! What does it spell? MILK! Go, Mamas! (If there was more room, I'd do a back handspring for you.)

Cate

Monday, August 27

Thanks, Cate and Stacy. I know I couldn't do this without you. I never imagined I'd breastfeed for more than 4 months, and here I am at 7. The one thing that really keeps me going (besides you) is how attached I've become to nursing Caleb—holding him close and soaking up the tenderness of it. I'm not ready to give that up yet.

Andrea

Tuesday, August 28

Here's an idea to inspire us. Let's make a list of the things we love about breastfeeding. I'll start:

1. Knowing I'm the only one who provides this perfect milk for Charlotte.
2. The quiet, beautiful intimacy of nursing.
3. Reconnecting with Charlotte after a busy day at work.

Cate

4. Bigger boobs!
5. Burning an extra 600 calories per day!
6. Guilt-free chocolate.

Stacy

7. When Caleb holds my finger as he nurses. I love that.

Andrea

8. When Ryan takes a break from nursing to look up and smile at me.

9. Immunity . . . he hasn't gotten a cold yet!

Anne

10. Saving money by not buying formula (justifies a new pair of espadrilles for me! Isn't that a fun word, espadrille?)

11. Diapers aren't as stinky.

Stacy

12. Bringing Charlotte into my bed first thing in the morning and nursing her.

13. Having an excuse to leave a meeting that runs past 5:30. Baby needs to eat!

14. The other day, Charlotte pinched her finger in the door and wanted to hold it against my breast to make it feel better. She just needed to get to second base and she was totally comforted. It was so sweet.

Cate

15. When Ella pretends to nurse her baby dolls.

16. Knowing breastmilk from "the source" is what Ryan loves best (still not fond of bottles).

Anne

17. Rubbing Caleb's forehead as he nurses.

18. How Caleb twirls my hair with his little fingers—it's the reason I keep my long mane!

Andrea

19. Let's not forget the pleasure of pumping in this beige, cinder-block ~~janitor closet~~ pumping palace. (Is it any wonder I'm quitting? I didn't get to enjoy half of this stuff! Maybe I'll get to savor the good stuff when I have another baby.)

Steph

Wednesday, August 29

Stephanie, you are a star for pumping so long! Here's one you can relate to:

20. Getting a break from work. Sure beats smoking outside in the rain.

Stacy

WHY DO WE DO IT?

It's no wonder the number-one reason new moms quit breast-feeding is because they return to work outside the home. When you're tired, overworked, and without a support group or convenient place to pump, it's only natural to find yourself thinking about how you could lighten the load. Even if you're fortunate enough to have a cushy pumping palace and a strong network of friends, you still have to juggle family, career, and all of life's other demands—so why endure the added hassle of lugging your pump to and from work each day? In our fast-food society, where even some hospitals and pediatrician's offices give away conveniently packaged formula, it can be all too tempting to stop breastfeeding.

FOUNTAIN OF YOUTH

If you've stuck with us this far, you probably don't really need to be convinced *why* breast is best, but it never hurts to be reminded. Experts across the board, from the American Academy of Pediatrics, the National Women's Health Information Center, the U.S. Department of Health and Human Services, the U.S. Breastfeeding Committee, major corporations, and even formula companies have conducted extensive research and published numerous documents advocating breastfeeding.

Human milk is a virtual miracle drug, helping to protect little ones from ear infections, allergies, asthma, dental problems, and diarrhea. Breastmilk also provides increased protection against RSV, multiple sclerosis, type 2 diabetes, obesity, several types of cancer, Crohn's and Hodgkin's diseases, respiratory infections, and SIDS. Studies even link breastmilk to increased cognitive development and higher IQ. This isn't to say that formula-fed babies are doomed to a life of misery and poor health (although some people might tell you so). The world is full of intelligent, healthy adults who were fed formula. Still, there's no question that breastmilk gives babies a gigantic jump-start on life. And what mom doesn't want to give her baby the very best?

Of course, breastfeeding is also good for *you*. Besides increasing your bra size and delaying the return of your period, breastfeeding helps you shed pregnancy pounds. Women who breastfeed exclusively burn *six hundred calories* per day. That's like getting in a good workout every day of the week—and you don't even have to break a sweat!

More importantly, when you breastfeed you're at lower risk for breast cancer, and the longer you breastfeed over your lifetime, the more your risk decreases. Breastfeeding also has a protective effect against osteoporosis and uterine, ovarian, cervical, and endometrial cancers.

In addition to the medical benefits, breastfeeding can be relaxing. Knowing that you "have to" sit down and snuggle your baby several times a day forces even the busiest of moms to slow down. Then your brain kicks in, manufacturing chemicals while you're nursing that actually calm you and give you a sense of well-being.

Is there anything breastmilk can't do? Next thing we know it will be credited with ending global warming and delivering world peace. Until then, we know that breast-feeding helps society economically and environmentally. A study by the Wisconsin State Breastfeeding Coalition revealed that if 75 percent of new moms breastfed their newborns, and 50 percent continued breastfeeding for at least six months, the total health-care cost savings in Wisconsin would be $31 million per year! According to the American Academy of Pediatrics, increased breastfeeding rates could decrease health-care costs by $3.6 billion per year in the United States. No wonder the U.S. Department of Health and Human Services established a "Blueprint for Action on Breastfeeding" and set a "Healthy People 2010" goal which calls for 50 percent of moms to continue breastfeeding for at least six months. With all the money we're saving the government, there should be a Milk Mama tax break!

THE FLIP SIDE

Despite understanding all the benefits, there are sure to be days when you wonder what you've gotten yourself into. Even if you are gung-ho about breastfeeding or actually enjoy pumping, there's no question that taking your pump or your baby with you wherever you go, worrying about your supply, and finding time to stick to a regular pumping routine isn't easy. And it's not just pumping that gets Milk Mamas frustrated. Nursing itself can be a pain, especially if you get cracked nipples, plugged ducts, or worse. And of course, there are plenty of moms who never get off to a good breastfeeding start after giving birth, so they don't find it to be a wonderful, blissful experience. Though we're often led to believe nursing will be easy, the truth is that it takes lots of practice, for both mom and baby. As one Mama said, "It takes two people, three hands, and thirty pillows to feed this child!" If it's time for you to return to work and breastfeeding feels like a chore, don't lose hope—you may still come to love it. But if nursing never clicks, yet you still nurse and/or pump, here's to you! You're the Milk Mama we admire most.

THE FINISH LINE

When you have days that make you consider giving your pump to Goodwill, think of one or two things you love about nursing. Like us, you'll probably find yourself thinking about the quiet, tender moments—how it feels to hold your baby close, to hear her soft breathing, to see her contentment. The fact that your breastmilk will protect her from ear infections is just the icing on the cake. Still, all moms have days when they simply need to remember why they started this journey in the first place. Set little goals for yourself and reach them one day at a time. If nothing else, try to have peace of mind knowing that you're helping to protect your baby by giving her the best food on earth. Push through and presevere—you'll be glad you did.

Friday, August 31

Just thought of another one:

21. Knowing every ounce my little Ryan has gained came from *my milk*.

Anne

(Ditto, Steph)

22. Having a good excuse to sit still and just be with Charlotte.
23. It's something *only I* can do. It's pure motherhood.
24. Nursing Charlotte while we take a bath together.
25. Feeling that my breasts are alive and serving their true purpose.

Cate

26. The look on my cat's face when I squirted him with breastmilk to get him off the coffee table.

27. Learning to bare my boobs without shame.

28. Freaking out my mother-in-law with my lack of modesty.

    Stacy

29. Listening to Ryan breathe as he nurses.

30. Holding him as he falls asleep at my breast.

    Anne

31. Meeting each other!

    Cate

· · ·

TWELVE

working from home

My path to becoming an IBM executive just took another detour! This morning I had a 5:30 A.M. conference call, which first of all is ridiculous. The meeting was called by a fancy-pants New York executive who thinks the whole world runs on East Coast time. (I feel really sorry for the people calling from California!) Wouldn't you know it— Charlotte woke up at 5:00! I held her on my lap, put on my headset, and dialed in. To join the call I had to "state my name, followed by the pound sign." I took the phone off mute just long enough to say my name, but at that moment, Charlotte started screaming her head off and pulling on the headset cord. So when they patched me into the call, it said, "Now joining conference . . . WAAAAAAHHH!!" Some man said, "Wow, they're recruiting them younger and younger these days." Of course I couldn't even pay attention to the call because (1) I was half-asleep, (2) I was trying to console Charlotte, (3) it was freaking me out to be nursing Charlotte while listening to people talk about how to better execute our go-to-market plans, and (4) I knew my manager would make some smart remark about the baby crying faux pas when I got into the office. Oh well . . . hope your week is going better than mine!

Cate

Monday, September 10

Cate,

I can totally relate. Since I work from home two days a week, I've had my share of mute button mishaps. Why is it that people are so much more understanding of a dog barking or a doorbell ringing in the background than a baby crying?

Andrea

P.S. Maybe no one knew that the "WAAAHH" was you (I mean Charlotte).

Monday, September 10

Unfortunately, my manager didn't even wait until I got into the office—she called me right after the conference call and asked if the crying baby was mine. What could I say?

Cate

Monday, September 10

Cate,

You should have said, "Yes, it was Charlotte. By the way, are you aware that most people don't have child care arranged at 5:30 in the frickin' morning?!" While we're on the subject, I had to work from home yesterday because George got his first cold over the weekend, and couldn't go to day care. He's better today—thank goodness, because I didn't get anything done yesterday (besides holding and soothing him). I am one stressed Mama. Andrea, I don't know how you do it 2 days a week.

Stacy

MIXED BLESSING

Many moms ease their transition back to work by arranging to work from home for some period of time. In today's flexible world, many scenarios are possible. You might start by working from home entirely when your baby is a newborn (and sleeps a lot—cross your fingers), then gradually spending more days at the office as he grows. If your employer is supportive, you may be able to continue working from home indefinitely, at least for a day or two per week. Flexibility is the key. Depending on your employer and the nature of your work, you may be able to ask for flextime, working when and where you want, as long as you're delivering results.

Especially in the beginning, working from home can seem like an ideal situation. You're not ready to hand over your baby to somebody else. If you're lucky, your baby sleeps just enough that you can still get work done (forget about "sleep when the baby sleeps"). You're there to kiss her toes and nurse her when she wakes up. You're there for the first smile, the first giggle, and the first time she grabs a rattle and shakes it.

However, working from home also has its challenges. When the love of your life is right there next to you cooing in her bouncy seat, it can be very hard to concentrate on work. You may feel guilty when you can't give her your full attention, which she's had throughout your maternity leave. Babies don't understand when you have a major deadline or an important conference call. Then again, maybe they do, because that's inevitably the moment when they have a poopy diaper blowout or a screaming, crying fit.

Some moms get a little stir-crazy at home, and miss the social interaction with coworkers. Many (old-fashioned, control-freak) managers demand face time—they want to be able to pop their head into your office at any given moment with a quick question. Your coworkers may look down upon you, either because they're jealous that they didn't have the opportunity to work from home when their kids were little or because they don't believe you're really *working*. It's common for moms with nontraditional work settings and schedules to feel (and be treated) like second-class citizens.

Fortunately, many working moms have paved the way for us. Together we are slowly but surely overcoming the negative attitudes about working moms (and dads too!) who boldly put family first, taking extended maternity (and paternity) leaves, working part-time and flexible schedules, job sharing, and working more from home, even if it means sacrificing near-term career advancement. (For more on flexible work options, see pages 307–13.) As more moms take this risk and prove that it's possible to be productive, effective, dependable, and committed regardless of hours or location, the "mommy track" label will go the way of the Selectric typewriter.

IT'S ALL ABOUT THE MUTE BUTTON

To make the most of a work-from-home job, here are some tips.

Get help.

- As your baby becomes more active, and especially if you have more than one child, arrange for child care in or near your house so that you can get work done, and still be there for your baby throughout the day. You might even be able to swap duty with other work-from-home or stay-at-home moms in your neighborhood or find a "mother's helper" (teenager) to help after school or during the summer.

Go shopping!
- Set up an official home office complete with desk, chair, computer, phone, all the essentials—this will help you get into the working mode.
- Get a good laptop computer and a high-speed Internet connection.
- Buy a headset for your phone so that your hands can be free to hold, nurse, burp, and diaper your baby when needed.
- Make sure the headset has a convenient mute button, for obvious reasons!
- You might also want a speaker phone (with mute!) for times when you need to listen to a call, but don't need to speak much.

Act the part.
- As tempting as it is to stay in your pajamas and bunny slippers, take the time to get dressed so that you feel more present and ready to work.

- Establish a regular working routine around your baby's feeding, sleeping, and waking habits—try to schedule your meetings and focused work time around this. Most likely, you'll get uninterrupted stretches of work done in the mornings, during naptime, or at night (or even on the weekends).

- Just because you're at home doesn't mean that you should also do the laundry, straighten up the house, and sweep the floors in addition to doing your "real" (paid) work plus caring for your baby. Prioritize your time, and put house chores last. Dust can wait.

- If you don't have a separate business phone line, answer your home phone just as you would at work, and make your home answering machine greeting professional.

Work smart.
- Plan your projects in bite-sized pieces so you can be productive and efficient in the time you do have to work.

- Communicate frequently with your manager and coworkers—overcommunicate, in fact, so that there's not doubt about your daily or weekly accomplishments. Make it a point to attend most or all staff or departmental meetings so your colleagues and boss don't forget that you're a valuable member of the team.

- If possible, negotiate for task- and result-oriented duties rather than putting in a set number of hours per week.

Take heed.

- When you're consumed with taking care of your baby and trying to get your work done, it can be all too easy to forget the importance of making time for yourself and your husband/partner (this goes for office workers too). Remember the airplane guideline: for the safety and security of your family, put your own oxygen mask on first before assisting others. It's hard to do, but you must find time to replenish your own energy and rejuvenate, whether this means a workout, a date night, girls' night out, sleeping in on Saturday, or just watching your favorite TV show.

- Prepare yourself for the fact that working from home is not always perfect. There will be days when your baby is sick or teething and you won't get anything accomplished. There will also be days when you feel stressed, guilty, pulled between work demands and your baby's needs, and just plain overwhelmed.

- Working from home will never be like working in an office. You'll have drool marks on your daily planner and milk drips on presentations, but most importantly, you'll be home with your little one!

Count your blessings.

- Be grateful for every moment with your baby. When you look back, you'll certainly remember your baby's bright eyes, chubby legs, and perfectly soft skin more than the e-mails you didn't get to or the deadline you missed.

Wednesday, September 12

Since we're on the subject, let me share my mute-button secret. Sometimes, when I'm on a conference call from home, I pretend to be on mute. Here's how it works. If Caleb is making a racket while my manager asks me a question, I purposely keep the mute button on. Then, while she's saying, "Andrea, did you hear the question?" I quickly quiet Caleb down or whisk him away to the next room, take the phone off mute, and say, "Oh, I was answering you but forgot that the mute button was on!" It doesn't always work, of course, but it was a life-saver just last week!

It's all smoke and mirrors,

Andrea

Wednesday, September 12

Hi. New mommy in the milk room! My name is Samantha. All the baby pictures on the wall are adorable! My daughter Sara just turned 8 weeks on Sunday, and Monday was my first day back. I'm not ready to be here again—can't get back into the groove of working (I'm an admin assistant for 2 VPs in Bldg. 26) because I feel like I'm missing half my heart without Sara! She's the cutest thing ever with her skinny little waist (from Dad) and big ol' double chin (from me). Ha. There's no lactation room in my bldg. but someone just told me about this one. Is it the only one? It takes me at least 10 minutes just to walk here, and I'm only "allowed" to be away from my desk for two 15-minute "breaks." I think I was sleepwalking on the way over—only got 4 hours of sleep (if you can call it that) last night. This whole infant + work thing feels IMPOSSIBLE—and exhausting. But I see that you guys are surviving—that's encouraging!

Sam

Wednesday, September 12

Welcome, Samantha! I'm Cate, Charlotte's mom. My heart always goes out to moms who are struggling through their first week back. We've all been there, and we totally understand. If you have time, read through the notebooks . . . you are in good company! I wish I had good news for you about the exhaustion you're feeling. I think all of us would agree that after having a baby, you adjust to living your life in a bit of a hazy daze.

Andrea,

I'll have to remember your mute-button trick next time I work from home! I'm trying to figure out why I don't work from home more often since my manager said it would be OK every once in a while (as long as there's no crying in the background on a conference call!). I think the problem is that when I'm at home I'm constantly aware of Charlotte in the next room reading books and playing peek-a-boo with the nanny or Chris. I start to feel jealous and resentful that I have to sit there doing e-mails and trying to concentrate on performance reviews for my team. Sometimes it feels easier to put some distance between me and Charlotte so that I don't feel so conflicted. But how sad is that?

Cate

Wednesday, September 12

Welcome, Samantha. Glad you found us. This is the best (and yes, only) lactation room at IBM.

Anne (Ryan and Ella's mom)

P.S. You guys, I ran into Stephanie in the parking lot this morning. She's officially pulled the plug on her pump, and she and Darren are both doing great. I told her we miss her, and she's always welcome to stop by the Palace and say hi (and escape from Dirk's smelly feet).

Wednesday, September 12

Hooray! Another Mama joins the club! To qualify for membership, you must be a sleep-deprived, frazzled milk goddess who is willing to write in the journal. A sense of humor and a picture of your baby are also required. So just bring a pic of Sara, and you're in!

Cate,

I know what you mean. Working from home is one of the hardest—and most enjoyable—things I do (well, besides trying to work and nurse!). I'm constantly torn between my desire to pay attention to Caleb and my work. I try not to do IBM stuff when he's awake, but sometimes it's impossible to avoid "urgent" e-mails and constant calls from my manager about a project that has to be completed TODAY. The more active Caleb gets, the harder it is to stay on top of my work. It totally stresses me out. Some days, I have back-to-back conference calls and I feel like I have to ignore him for hours! It kills me. When he was four months old, I was on a call and Caleb was crying his head off. I couldn't go on mute because I was leading the call. So I strapped him in his car seat (still screaming) and

put him in the other room and closed the door for the last 10
minutes of the call. That image will haunt me forever, and
it's making me cry just thinking about it. I'll never forget
picking him up after the call, *both* of us sobbing. That was
one of those days when I felt like I wasn't a good mom *or* a
good employee.

   Guilt ridden, Andrea

Wednesday, September 12

Wow. That story says it all. I feel like I should give you advice, but I don't know what to say. Is it better to cut off the call
when everyone knows it's because Caleb is crying? If you do
that, your manager might be even less supportive of you
working from home. But it doesn't seem right to put a conference call before your baby. It's not fair to either of you.
Maybe it would be best if you could have a nanny, babysitter,
help from a neighbor, or even a mother's helper (after school
or during the summer). Lucky for me, I've never had to deal
with that situation because I like coming into the office. I need
that separation from my kids. I still miss them, of course, but
I have no desire to try to work *and* be home with them. I hope
that doesn't make me sound like less of a mom, but it's just
who I am and I've come to peace with it.

   Hey, Samantha! Glad our Milk Mama Club is growing.

Tell us more about Sara! Where does she go during the day? Also, make yourself at home and help yourself to the community soap, drying racks, and paper towels. We're still waiting for the La-Z-Boy recliners and calming, trickling water fountain to arrive.

Stacy, a.k.a Jugs, Dorm Mother, Resident Expert, and Mommy (to Colby and George)

Thursday, September 13

Andrea,

That story is a heartbreaker. I give you credit for toughing it out, even when your manager is calling constantly and Caleb and IBM are stretching you to the limit. Hang in there. And remember all the good times—when you get to be there when he wakes up and take little breaks to hug and tickle him. He's lucky and so are you.

Cate

P.S. Charlotte can pull herself to standing. Now when I go to her crib in the mornings she stands there and smiles at me, so proud of herself.

Friday, September 14

Thanks, everyone, for the welcome. FINALLY I've almost made it through the first week, but barely. At lunchtime in the cafeteria, I was digging through my purse for my wallet but grabbed Sara's giraffe rattle instead. It was like getting the wind knocked out of me. PLEASE tell me it gets easier.

Sara goes to Children's World in north Boulder. It seems really nice, or at least I keep telling myself that!

Have a great weekend.

Sam

Monday, September 17

I don't mean to fill this whole notebook with the play-by-play of my work-from-home issues, but I need to set the record straight. I don't want to leave the impression that working from home is all stress and tears. For the most part, it is an experience I wouldn't trade for the world. I'm grateful that I can be there to nurse Caleb throughout the day and feel like I'm not missing so many of his baby days. Because I've helped raise my older kids, Cody and Sierra, I know all too well how fast time passes. Of course, I'd rather not have to work on those days, but I'm glad I can contribute to the family income *and* be with Caleb.

But here's the catch. My manager recently hinted that I won't be able to work from home forever. She wants me back in the office every day, but I'm not ready to give my precious Caleb time up. Actually, I'm thinking about asking to go part-time but I don't know what I'll do if she says no.

Andrea

P.S. Go, Charlotte! I can't believe she's learning to stand. Caleb is just starting to army crawl, a few inches at a time. We call him our little wounded soldier because he drags his legs. Cute!

Monday, September 17

Andrea,

If your manager says no, hit her over the head with the latest issue of *Working Mother* magazine. IBM is once again named one of the top 10 best companies for working moms. I'll bring the mag in for you. Maybe instead of hitting your manager, you could discreetly tape the article to her door!

Stacy

P.S. Andrea, congrats to Caleb on crawling! George is starting to crawl too. Maybe they can enlist in the army together! Or not.

Monday, September 17

If IBM is one of the top 10, God help the moms who work for companies that didn't even make the top 100 list!

Anne

Monday, September 17

Andrea,

I envy you. I could never work from home or ask for part-time unless I found another job. All I've done since college is admin work. My degree in poli sci hasn't gotten me very far (although I can debate foreign policy with the best of 'em)!

The F word (flexibility) is totally missing from my job. I might as well be wearing one of those ankle monitors for criminals on home detention. I can't go beyond a 15-foot radius of my desk!

Sam

Tuesday, September 18

Brought in the mag. Check it out!

S

Tuesday, September 18

This article is telling. IBM scores well for on-site day care (when will Boulder get with the program?!) and flexible work options (hello, Andrea's manager). But what about the perks at other companies? Some companies have 6 weeks' paid paternity leave, which isn't particularly useful in my situation, but is still cool! And there's sick-child care, before- and after-school care, and my favorite—take-home meals! Now, *that's* a working mother's dream!

Anne

Tuesday, September 18

UPDATE: I asked my manager for part-time and she said she'd think about it! Keep your fingers crossed.

A

P.S. I'll take rosemary-rubbed pork tenderloin, garlic mashed potatoes, mixed green salad with balsamic vinaigrette, crème brulée, a jar of green beans, and some Cheerios.

Wednesday, September 19

Well, it's not looking good for me to go part-time. My manager told me my job can't be done in part-time hours (which is true), and she's not going to hire anyone else. I mentioned the possibility of hiring a contractor (no), finding someone to job share with (slim chance), but I can't think of anyone to job share with. Anyone game?

Andrea

P.S. She also told me I can only work from home (Thurs. and Fri.) until the end of the year, when Caleb will be almost 1. I'm so depressed.

Thursday, September 20

Andrea,

I'm so sorry to hear that. I wish I could job share with you but our jobs are so different! Maybe you should check with HR and the Women's Networking Group to see if your perfect job-share mate is out there somewhere.

Cate

Thursday, September 20

Andrea,

Just when you thought your dating days were over, you now have to court a job-share match. Try placing a personal ad: heartbroken ~~SWF~~ MWF with adorable infant son seeks job-share partner. Must be intelligent, hardworking, and telepathic. Must also crave liberation from insane 50+ hour workweek/corporate shackles. Workaholics need not apply.

Stacy

Friday, September 21

Stacy,

That ad is hilarious! After reading it, I couldn't get "The Piña Colada Song" out of my head! You know the one? "If you like piña coladas, getting caught in the rain . . ." Well, since I couldn't stop singing the song, I made up some new lyrics:

If you like pumping breastmilk, and still using your brain.

Want to be with your baby, and find full-time working
a pain.

If you are changing diapers at midnight, and tired of IBM
red tape,

You're the job-share partner I've looked for, work with me,
and escape.

What do you think??

Cate

THIRTEEN

. . .

business - class blues

Monday, September 24

Oh NO! My day started with my manager telling me I need to fly to New York for a meeting THIS THURSDAY! She needs me there in her place so she can go to her mother-in-law's funeral. I don't know what to do. I'm in shock. Can I possibly say no? I would have to leave at the crack of dawn Wednesday and get home late Friday night. I know it's not that long, but I've never been away from Charlotte overnight. Help! How is it even going to work with the pumping??? Any tips from the pros?

Cate

Monday, September 24

Cate,

Wish I could go for you! I mean, I know it would be hard . . . but look at the bright side! What I wouldn't give for room service and a full night's sleep. I'm thinking bubble baths and HBO. Ahhhhh.

Anne

Monday, September 24

Cate,

Pumping while traveling is a pain in the butt for sure. I did it when Colby was 5 months. I was gone 4 nights. I brought my regular pump (of course), and also a backup hand pump for the plane and to use during meeting breaks (in case I couldn't find a room with a power outlet). I carried my milk home in one of those collapsible coolers, using a bunch of ice packs. Since you're only going to be gone a couple days, it may be easier to just pump and dump. Since Charlotte eats solid foods, maybe your nanny/husband can ration your breastmilk while you're gone. I think Anne's right—once you're away, you might enjoy having some Cate time.

Stacy

Monday, September 24

EEK! From this point on, I forbid anyone to use the expression "pump and dump." I can't bear the thought of it. Maybe if I were a dairy cow like you, Jugs, I would feel differently.

Andrea

Monday, September 24

Hang on, you're all assuming I'm going on the trip. I'm actually considering telling my manager no. Political suicide? This meeting just doesn't seem that important, honestly. Plus (shhhh!) the other thing is that I really want to get pregnant again. We just started trying last month, but with Charlotte it took us over two years to get pregnant. And of course I think I'll be ovulating when I'm gone. Just my luck!

Cate

Tuesday, September 25

Cate,

I'm afraid pushing back would land you in a career cul-de-sac. May not be worth it. I've got one word for you: sleep.

Anne

P.S. I'm excited for you to get pregnant, Cate! Remind me next month—I have a couple steamy movies you can borrow (R rated, don't worry)! In fact, you can have them—they've already gotten me into enough trouble.

Tuesday, September 25

I know I need my sleep. But I don't think I'll be able to sleep in a strange hotel room 2,000 miles away from Charlotte. Still, you're probably right about how I'll be perceived if I say no. I can imagine my performance review . . . "Well, Cate, when we asked you to step up, you weren't a team player showing passion for the business. . . ." Cripes. I guess I'll go confirm my reservation.

Cate

P.S. I'll take you up on your movie offer.

Tuesday, September 25

Hi, everyone. Cate, sorry to hear about your dilemma. I've never been on a business trip in my life. It's hard enough being away during the day. I'm really struggling. Sara has started smiling whenever I walk in the room, and that makes me miss her all the more when I'm here staring at a computer (or breastpump!) instead of her.

Sam

Tuesday, September 25

Sam and Cate,

Hang in there. Not that I'm one to give advice—I still struggle too, and Caleb is 8 months old now! If my manager told me
to go on a business trip, I'd be a bundle of nerves. I can barely
hack pumping here at IBM, let alone some faraway hotel!

Andrea

Tuesday, September 25

Guess who? I stopped in on my way to the cafeteria to see
how you're doing and to say hi. I'm officially done pumping.
Freedom! Darren's doing great and is chugging formula like
it's going out of style (which it kind of is, but oh well). I'm
glad to see that a new Mama has taken over my spot on the
drying rack. Miss you guys. Thanks for everything.

Steph

P.S. I moved Darren's picture to the Graduate Wall.

Tuesday, September 25

Cate,

We will miss you while you're in NY! Try to enjoy yourself. Don't be doing e-mail at night in your hotel room—
pay-per-view movie time! You must report back on Monday.

Bon voyage, Stacy

LEAVING ON A JET PLANE

For many of us, there was a time when business trips were a treat. Flying to a new city or exotic part of the world, enjoying a break from your routine, staying in a nice hotel, and getting paid to eat out had some definite appeal. All of that changes once you're a mom. Now even Hawaii or Kuala Lumpur don't sound as inviting if you can't take your baby along. It's hard enough being away from your baby all day while you're at work. But when you can't see her for days at a time, you miss her in a whole different way, and new worries arise. You wonder, will your baby be OK without you during the night? Will your husband get up to comfort her, or will he let her cry? Do you have enough milk stored in the freezer to last while you're gone? If not, will she reject formula? What if she goes on a bottle strike? What if she weans herself while you're away? Will she remember you when you get home? Plus, the whole time you're gone, you feel as if you're forgetting something important, like your laptop . . . or even worse, you just feel naked. Then, out of habit, you find yourself looking in the rearview mirror, and your heart skips a beat when the car seat's gone, until you realize, sadly, that you're in Boston driving a rental car.

OCCUPIED

On top of the emotional strain of a business trip, there are practical questions about where and how you'll pump. If a short flight is in your future, you probably won't need to worry about pumping in an airplane bathroom (pray there's no mechanical or weather delay!), but you may have to pump in the airport before you depart. Pumping in an airport bathroom isn't exactly appealing, but it's better than doing it in the tiny, stinky plane bathroom with blue toilet water, a miniature sink, and a line of people outside wondering what the heck is taking so long. That said, if you do have to pump on the plane, you can do it! After all, if people manage to have sex in airplane bathrooms, then certainly it should be possible for you and your breastpump to get cozy in there. Before going in, tell a flight attendant what you're up to so that she/he can help divert passengers to the other restroom. Unfortunately, there's no electrical outlet in airplane bathrooms, so to pump there you'll need battery power or a hand pump.

Don't be caught unprepared like one Mama we read about. She expected a short flight, but was delayed for several hours on the tarmac. The longer she sat, the more full and uncomfortable her breasts became, but she needed a power outlet in order to use her electric pump. Finally, she pressed her call button and spoke to a flight attendant who told her she could use the outlet in the galley. She was relieved until she discovered that her clunky pump plug didn't fit in the outlet! Desperate, she asked for help again. The flight attendant made an announcement asking if anyone happened to have a power strip or extension cord. Ding! A miracle: someone did, and the story had a happy ending. All of this to say that when you travel, prepare for the worst and always have a backup plan.

CARRY-ON LUGGAGE

Refrigerated breastmilk stays fresh for up to eight days, so if you're going to be gone less than a week, there's probably no need to freeze your milk. Bring a collapsible cooler and enough freezer packs to keep everything cold while you travel. Once you reach your destination, you'll need to refreeze the freezer packs so you can use them again when you fly home. Most hotels will let you use space in their restaurant freezer. At the very least, call ahead to make sure there's a refrigerator in your room. You can turn the minibar into a breastmilk bar! If there's no refrigerator in your room, check to see if the hotel has a minifridge available for rent. Otherwise, you'll become very acquainted with the ice machine. One Milk Mama repeatedly filled her trash can with ice to keep her milk bags cold. Another got creative and used her rental car as a refrigerator (that's the bright side of being in Boston during a snowstorm). If you're traveling overseas, be sure to bring a battery pack or buy a power converter for your pump. Be forewarned, though: even if you buy a high-quality converter, your pump probably won't have as much oomph as it does in the States. As a result, you may have to pump a little more frequently to keep your supply up.

If you're feeling overwhelmed by the idea of lugging your breastpump along with your laptop, coat, purse, cooler, and luggage, you could consider renting a breastpump from a local hospital at your destination. Call the hospital ahead of time to reserve the pump, and ask for pump details so you know whether it will work with your parts. If so, bring your own shields, tubes, bottles, and other doodads, and leave your bulky, heavy pump behind. It might be a good idea to bring a backup hand pump in case there's a flight delay or other mishap.

LONG-TERM PARKING

If you're going on a long business trip, hopefully the sadness you'll feel while away from your baby will be lessened by knowing that he can still have your bottled breastmilk while you're away (providing you have enough stored). Also by going to the trouble of pumping while traveling, you'll maintain your supply so you can continue breastfeeding when you get home, for as long as you and your baby like. Often, the biggest challenge for moms who travel for long periods of time is having enough breastmilk for their babies to drink while they're gone. If you have a healthy breastmilk stockpile in the freezer, this won't be a big concern. If not, add early-morning or late-night pumping sessions to your routine before you leave so you can store extra milk. If you don't have a frozen stash or enough forewarning to build one, you can ship frozen milk from wherever you go. After you pump, freeze your milk in the hotel's freezer. Then, pack your milk in a Styrofoam cooler with ice packs or dry ice and drop it off at FedEx. If your milk arrives thawed, it can be refrigerated and used within twenty-four hours. It can't be refrozen, though.

A WORD ABOUT DRY ICE

If you want to ensure your milk will arrive frozen, you can use dry ice. Dry ice is frozen carbon dioxide, and at −109 degrees Fahrenheit it will definitely keep your milk frozen! But while shipping or traveling with dry ice may sound like a good idea at first, it's enough of a hassle that it's impractical for most moms.

If you want to give it a go, start by looking online or in the phone book to find out where to buy the ice. You may only find it in major metropolitan areas. There's usually a minimum purchase of ten pounds required, which costs about ten dollars. Throw some mittens in your briefcase— you'll need them to handle the dry ice.

The maximum weight you can carry onto an airplane is four pounds, and it must be packaged in a ventilated container. You can drop a ten-pound slab on the floor to get smaller pieces. Don't worry; the billowing-fog haunted-house effect only occurs when hot liquid is poured over dry ice. Four pounds of ice will keep your milk frozen for approximately twelve hours. Packing newspaper or other filler around the ice helps it last as long as possible. If you're driving rather than flying, keep the dry ice in the trunk, or if it's inside the car, be sure to keep the vents outside open or windows cracked. Carbon dioxide has no smell or color, but can be deadly if inhaled in large amounts. Take a break from driving and get fresh air immediately if you experience any of these symptoms: nausea, dizziness, headache, difficulty breathing, rapid pulse, or fatigue.

To ship dry ice, FedEx recommends packing it in a sturdy Styrofoam cooler with packing material to minimize movement. The cooler must then be packed inside a thick cardboard box. Anything over five pounds of dry ice requires a

Dangerous Goods label, which FedEx will provide. There is no surcharge for dry-ice shipments. Priority overnight service means you can drop your frozen milk off in the evening by 6:00 P.M. for a 10:30 A.M. arrival. Still, the FedEx guideline is to include enough dry ice to keep your shipment frozen for up to thirty hours. Ten pounds will keep it frozen for twenty-four hours, so you may want more than ten pounds of dry ice just be to sure. Be ready for sticker shock: it will cost well over fifty dollars to overnight a box of this weight.

BABY ON BOARD

Given the difficulty and heartache of leaving your baby at home when you travel, the inconvenience of pumping while away, and hassle and expense of dry ice, you might consider bringing your baby with you on your trip. Some employers are more accommodating of the idea than others. It's encouraging to know that, according to the Travel Industry Association of America, more than 32 million business trips a year include children, which is nearly a 100 percent increase over the last decade.

Of course, you'd also need to bring your nanny, relative, or husband to care for your baby while you're working. This means forking over cash for an extra plane ticket, but sometimes peace of mind is well worth the price. Another option would be to arrange for a local babysitter. Some hotels have child-care programs, and others have lists of employees or locals who provide babysitting services. If these aren't available, you can look for a bonded babysitting service in the area. We read about one Mama who phoned the hotel concierge, found out she was a mother, and asked if she could use her babysitter during the business trip. Of course, leaving your baby with a stranger in a strange city can feel scary, so do as much background checking as possible, and ask all the right questions about the person's experience and qualifications. If you bring your baby along, and the business trip location is a fun one, you could always extend your stay and make a family vacation out of your trip.

business travel checklist

☐ Breastpump—electric and/or hand pump (Triple-check that all pump parts are accounted for!)
☐ Freezer packs
☐ Milk storage bags
☐ Cooler—soft-sided collapsible type, or Styrofoam if you'll be shipping it

☐ Battery pack, car adapter, or power adapters if you're traveling internationally

☐ Gloves, packing material (and plenty of money) if you're
using dry ice

☐ Pictures of your baby!

Wednesday, September 26

I wonder how Cate's doing on her big excursion. I didn't
want to bring this up yesterday, but my biggest fear about
going on a trip without Caleb would be that the plane would
crash and Caleb would grow up without a mommy. I know
there's greater chance that I could get hit by the Schwan's
truck on the way home, but still . . . I have a fear of flying—
not so much that I won't do it, but enough that I worry like
crazy. I start thinking about whether Roger would find
someone else, and if so she could NEVER love Caleb as
much as I do. If I ever have to go on a business trip, Roger
and Caleb are coming with me!

Andrea

Wednesday, September 26

I wonder whether IBM would let you bring your family
along. My friend, who is also a single mom, asked if she

could bring her mom along to watch her infant son while she attended a recognition event. Her request went up to the top HR executive, who sent her the most infuriating e-mail—I have to bring it in for you to read. I saved it because I thought it was so appalling. What are single moms supposed to do? And my friend was a top performer, that's why she was invited to the event.

ARGH, Anne

Thursday, September 27

OK, here's the e-mail. Read it and weep, girls.

Anne

To: Brenda McCormick
Subject: Re: Recognition event in Palm Springs

Dear Brenda,

With respect to your inquiry regarding whether or not a nursing mother could bring her child and caregiver to "Top Performers Club," the consensus is that this would not qualify as a justifiable reason for an exception to be granted.

There is a lactation room available for nursing mothers that has a freezer/refrigerator which can be used to store breastmilk. Last year, several nursing mothers stored their milk and then shipped it to their babies at home.

As this is a business event, it would not be appropriate for any employee to bring a child and caregiver to Palm Springs.

Remember, the employee's attendance at TPC is ultimately his choice.

Regards,
Karen Nichols, VP, Human Resources

Thursday, September 27

OMG! Tell me that is not real! And from a woman?! That letter is so cold it gives me the chills. (Or is it this freezing room?)

Sam

Thursday, September 27

It's not as if your friend was going to set up an Exer-Saucer and bouncy seat in the middle of the meeting room! Give me a break. What *would* be a justifiable reason for an exception?

Stacy

Thursday, September 27

My favorite part is when Karen said, "attendence at TPC is ultimately *his* choice!" The whole thing reads like an impersonal form letter. Obviously Karen doesn't have a clue what a hassle it is to ship breastmilk, not to mention the expense. My friend Brenda looked into it briefly. In the end, she decided to boycott the event.

Anne

Thursday, September 27

Good for her!

Sam

Monday, October 1

Welcome back, Cate!

Guess what happened over the weekend! Caleb crawled out of the bathroom while I was drying my hair. I looked around and he was gone! It struck me that he can choose to go away from me now. I'm not ready for that!

Andrea

Monday, October 1

I survived! I am so glad to be home. I snuggled with Charlotte all weekend long. I was expecting a big smiley homecoming, but it was totally uneventful, like I had just been in the other room for five minutes! I was kind of sad. . . . It reminded me that she's used to me being gone. But the good thing is that she was fine. The frozen milk supply lasted, and I brought home 63 ounces! OK, so that's how much Stacy pumps on a daily basis, but it was pretty exciting for me. Charlotte is nursing just like normal, Chris seems to have bonded more with her, and he even taught her how to wave bye-bye! He told me he has a new appreciation for all the things I do, especially waking up to feed Charlotte in the middle of the night.

Cate

Monday, October 1

Yea, Cate! You did it! What about your assignment? What movie did you watch?

Stacy

Monday, October 1

I was too tired to watch a movie. Besides, I'm so out of it I didn't even recognize any of the titles (or half the actors). I opted for a bubble bath and a ridiculously expensive chardonnay from the minibar (more room for my breastmilk bags!). It was nice to have some quiet time, I must admit.

Cate

Tuesday, October 2

Cate,

How did the pumping and milk transport go?

Andrea

Tuesday, October 2

Pumping was a hassle, but I did it! The hardest part wasn't the travel, it was the all-day meeting on Thursday. The presentations were all running long, we were an hour off schedule, and the facilitator asked if it was OK with everyone if we just had a working lunch. NO! I raised my hand and explained that my breasts were bursting. Just kidding! I said there was some urgent business I had to take care of, and excused myself for 20 minutes.

Thankfully, I never had to pump on the airplane. I pumped in the airport bathroom before I got on the plane, then didn't have to pump again until I arrived.

I carried my milk back on the plane, no problem. All except the couple ounces I drank in my morning coffee! (There was only powder nondairy creamer in the room.) Have you ever tasted your breastmilk? It's supersweet!

Cate

Tuesday, October 2

Ewwwww. I can't imagine.

Stacy

Tuesday, October 2

I totally have! It's delicious, and I don't even like milk!

Anne

Wednesday, October 3

It seems so weird to drink your own breastmilk, but why? Your baby drinks it all the time. I put a drop on my wrist and tasted it a few times when Caleb was refusing a bottle (sure enough, the milk was sour!) but I've never been adventurous enough to take a full swig.

Andrea

Wednesday, October 3

You made me so curious, I just tasted some of my milk. I can't believe how sweet it is! No wonder Sara loves it so much!

Sam

Thursday, October 4

They say vanilla ice cream is the number-one favorite flavor—because it tastes like breastmilk! I wouldn't know—still can't bring myself to taste my milk.

Stacy

Thursday, October 4

Stacy,

Where do you come up with this stuff? You are a breastmilk encyclopedia.

Anne

Thursday, October 4

My favorite ice cream flavor is Rocky Road. Does that mean my mother fed me lumpy chocolate formula?!

Sam

FOURTEEN

• • •

indecent exposure

Monday, October 8

Hi, all. Hope everyone had a great weekend. Mondays are so hard. After being with our babies all weekend, it's back to fluorescent lights and plastic horns on our breasts. How depressing is that?

Sam

Monday, October 8

I think my breastpump misses me on weekends. She gets all my attention during the workweek and is quickly cast aside on weekends. She spent this past weekend locked in the trunk of my car. Poor thing.

Cate

Monday, October 8

Mine spent the weekend here in this lovely room. I think she growled at me when I walked in this morning.

Anne

Monday, October 8

I don't feel sorry for my pump—she gets more of my time and attention than even my dogs, Harley and Sugar. In fact, since we spend so much time with our pumps, we should give them names. How about Betty the Breastpump?

Andrea

Tuesday, October 9

Good idea! I think I'll call mine Sally the Suckinator! Or maybe Molly the Milk Pump.

Stacy

Tuesday, October 9

Thought of a few more: Madame Medela, Polly the Pump In Style, Infant Imposter. No, I'm going to name her Mrs. Beasley, after my favorite doll when I was a kid.

Cate

Tuesday, October 9

You are *not* going to believe what happened to me this morning! I was in a team meeting because I'm the official note-taker. The meeting went on and on, and I kept hoping for a break, knowing I needed to pump. My boss whispered to me, "I think you're leaking." I was mortified. There were nine people in the room, and there I was with two wet circles on my shirt. One woman handed me some tissues. At first I thought she wanted me to dab my shirt—as if that would help. Then she motioned to me that I should stuff them in my bra. Like I'm going to reach inside my shirt right there at the conference table! But I couldn't just get up and leave (God forbid—not with my boss). . . . All I wanted to do was pump, which totally made the leaking worse! By the time the meeting ended, the small circles were big bull's-eyes! Hope your day's going better than mine.

Sam

P.S. I'm naming my pump Lucy the Leak Levy.

Tuesday, October 9

Oh, Sam! Every nursing mom has leaky incidents. Maybe mine will make you feel a little better. Whenever my husband and I have sex (a rarity), milk shoots from my breasts. By now, it's more of a "leak," but in the early months after giving birth, it was like a geyser! The first time it happened,

I was so embarrassed (and surprised)! My husband didn't know what hit him! This little talent of mine doesn't exactly enhance our sex life, but at least my leaks are private. Too bad your evil boss had to be the one to notice yours. That must have been awful. I have a whole box of breastpads in my office—right next to the staples, paper clips, and condoms (kidding!). I don't really use them anymore (the breastpads!), so I'll bring them in for you.

Hang in there, Stacy

Whenever you mix bodily fluids with a public setting, you're bound to have embarrassing moments. Think about it this way: Compared to getting your period unexpectedly in junior high and doctors and nurses peering at your privates during childbirth, leaking breastmilk is a walk in the park. We are mammals, after all. We can't control everything our bodies do. Take solace in knowing that your girlfriends have all been there. It's nothing to be ashamed of. Bodily functions aren't the most popular water-cooler or cocktail-party subjects, but they shouldn't be taboo either. Throughout pregnancy, labor, pumping, and working, it's much easier to cope when we share with our girlfriends . . . everything from losing our mucous plugs to the consistency of our babies' poop.

Tuesday, October 9

No way! I thought I was the only one who spurted a fountain of breastmilk during hanky-panky. Sam, here's my leaky incident story. . . . It happened a couple months ago, and it's a different type of leaking. I was in my office finalizing some charts before a meeting when I felt something leaking—not in my shirt but in my underwear. Yikes! I looked down and—sure enough—I had started my period. Not just any period, the *postpartum gush*. Stained pants, stained chair, and my meeting was starting in 10 minutes. Thank God IBM has free tampons in all the women's restrooms (isn't that amazing?!). The only thing I could do was tie my blazer around my waist (quite the fashion statement), go to the meeting and give my presentation. Eighth grade all over again! What a joy it is to be female.

Cate

Tuesday, October 9

Cate,

I can't believe you didn't tell us about that before! That's why we have this notebook—for the inside scoop on all the stuff no one tells you, and you didn't know to ask. Then again, I guess I could have written about it—my first postpartum period was a doozy, too! Thank God it happened at home. It's sort of like when you first come home from the hospital and all nine periods that you missed come out at once! Why didn't our moms warn us about this?

Andrea

Wednesday, October 10

Happy Hump (or Pump) Day!

You're right. Sorry I didn't disclose earlier, but I was SO embarrassed! I hereby swear that I will tell you all the Milk Mama tips. And Charlotte, too, someday. Maybe when she's pregnant, I'll just give her a copy of these spiral notebooks!

Cate

Wednesday, October 10

Your embarrassing story makes me want to wear a double-thick maxipad with wings every day to work! Hopefully your warning will help me prevent another public humiliation.

Sam

TELL IT LIKE IT IS

Throughout your breastfeeding "career," there are bound to be times when you'll have to excuse yourself to pump when it's not convenient. While your first inclination is probably to make a generic excuse ("I have to go take care of something"), sometimes that just doesn't cut it. Others may question why you need to go right now, or wonder what could be more important than a 2:00 P.M. deadline. In these situations, you'll have to tell it like it is, which can be awkward. It's not every day we say the words "breast," "breastpump," "breastmilk," or "breastfeed" in conversation with our bosses, coworkers, or clients. But we have found that once you say the word "breast," people are quick to excuse you. Say it out loud. Don't whisper. It's nothing to be ashamed of—in fact you should be proud.

Wednesday, October 10

I know! Instead of giving our kids copies of these notebooks, we could help countless working moms avoid embarrassing moments by turning these into a book!

Andrea

Wednesday, October 10

Andrea,

I had that same thought myself, but I don't know the first thing about writing a book! Plus, who has time? Still, it really is a good idea. I could have used a book like this when I was getting ready to go back to work. You're a writer, aren't you?

Cate

Wednesday, October 10

With a full-time job, a baby, and two older kids, I'm completely maxed out. Still, it's fun to dream! How cool would it be if we created a book that helped other moms in the same way these notebooks have helped us?! Next thing we know, it will be a MAJOR MOTION PICTURE!

Andrea

Thursday, October 11

Starring Dolly Parton!

Anne

Thursday, October 11

Dolly's too old. With special effects these days, I'm sure they could cut and paste Dolly's breasts onto Sarah Jessica Parker.

Stacy

	Friday, October 12

Forget Hollywood, ladies. HELLO BROADWAY! *Milk: The Musical!*

Cate

	Friday, October 12

Yes! Can't you just see a big dance number where we wear lederhosen and sing, "The halls are alive with the sound of breastpumps!!!"

Stacy

CAUGHT IN THE ACT

In addition to leaks big and small, another embarrassing situation common to working moms is when a coworker barges in on a pumping session. One Milk Mama had just returned from maternity leave and was pumping in her office with the door securely locked. Being new to pumping, she had taken her bulky sweater completely off so she could see what she was doing. About five minutes into pumping, she heard male voices outside the door, and then a key in the lock. "No! No!" she yelled, "Don't come in!" But it was too late. She was face-to-face with two maintenance men who had come to do a routine check on her smoke alarm. They hadn't bothered to knock because they had been told she was still out on leave. The men made a quick exit, but not before our friend burst into tears. From that point on, she always put a sign on her door when she pumped and, just in case, she kept her shirt on!

Monday, October 15

Right now, as I pump, there is a MAN right outside the door fixing a toilet in the bathroom! I was already hooked up when I heard him ask a woman leaving the restroom if anyone else was in here. She said no, and in he came. I'm so scared he'll hear my pump and open the door to see what's making the noise. How long can it take to fix a toilet? I have to get back to my desk, but I don't want to just appear in the bathroom with a bunch of milky pump parts.

Why me? Tick-tock.

Sam

Ten minutes later, he's finally gone!

Monday, October 15

I guess that's a downside of having our pumping palace attached to the women's restroom! Let's hijack one of those yellow "Caution—Wet Floor" triangle stands and make a "Milk Mamas Pumping"—No Men Allowed! sign.

Stacy

Monday, October 15

"Men" and "pumping" don't even belong in the same sentence, and definitely not the same room! I don't even like to pump in front of my husband. It's just weird to have him see me sitting on our bed hunched over, with plastic funnels attached to my breasts, and my nipples stretching six inches. Not even my best sexy lingerie can erase that image.

Cate

Tuesday, October 16

Where my girlfriend works, they set up a small table and chair in the handicapped stall of the bathroom. First of all, *gross*—pumping two feet from a public toilet! Second, how private is that? The lock doesn't even work on the stall, so she has to hold her foot up against the door to keep it closed while she pumps. I guess we should count our blessings.

Anne

Tuesday, October 16

Anne,

I can't believe your friend has to pump in a bathroom stall. At least it's more private than pumping in a ski lodge cafeteria. My friend had to do that last winter because there were no power outlets in the bathroom. She found one in the eating area and created a little pumping fort, piling up ski jackets around her. I'm sure people were wondering what she was doing, but she figured she wouldn't be seeing them again, and tried to act like it was no big deal. Can anyone top that?

Andrea

P.S. What are your kiddos going to be for Halloween?

Tuesday, October 16

I can top it—I pumped in one of the viewing rooms in a funeral home at my grandmother's funeral. Thank God there was no body around (ha) but I was sure I could hear Nanna rolling over in her grave!

Stacy

P.S. Colby is going to be Batman and George is going to be Curious George, of course! I think I'll go as a chicken with my head cut off—no costume required! Ha. ~~MOO~~! BOO!

FIFTEEN

• • •

brain drain

Is it possible that my brain cells are escaping through my breastmilk? Last night, I forgot to put my pumped milk in the fridge (had to dump all 7.5 ounces) and this morning I totally spaced out an 8:00 meeting with my manager. Am I ever going to feel like myself again?

Andrea

Monday, October 22

I'm so glad I'm not the only one. I feel like I have a chronic case of amnesia! Or a case of Half-heimer's—half the time I can't even remember the simplest things. . . . Did I already shampoo my hair? Did I close the garage door? Did I remember my freezer packs?

Cate

Monday, October 22

How many kids do I have again?

Stacy

LOST YOUR KEYS AGAIN?

Like the infamous '80s ad campaign that showed a fried egg to depict a person's brain on drugs, a pregnant mom's brain often feels similarly scrambled during and after pregnancy. Most books tell you that short-term memory loss is worst during the third trimester but disappears a couple months after you give birth. Don't count on it. Even after you greet your bundle of joy, you'll probably find yourself needing lists to remember everything from doctor's appointments to buying more wet wipes for the diaper bag. Then, of course, you'll find yourself wondering where you put your lists. One mom described the feeling as "Etch A Sketch brain"— she'd mentally jot tasks down throughout the day, only to find them suddenly wiped out and gone forever with the slightest "shake-up." This kind of forgetfulness goes beyond asking yourself what you're looking for in the refrigerator. It's when you can't remember where the refrigerator *is* that you know there's a problem. There are days when you feel as if your brain were clouded with a milky fog. You can't concentrate or make decisions as quickly as before you were pregnant. Concepts that were once easily understandable now seem as though they came straight from a calculus textbook. On top of it all, you're bumbling around exhausted, and juggling feelings that swing wildly at the speed of light—frustration, anxiety, guilt, impatience, and depression one second . . . joy, pride, gratitude, delight, and self-confidence the next.

THE BOOBY TRAP

booby trap
Pronunciation: 'bü-bē 'trap
Function: noun
  1: a trap for the unwary or unsuspecting : PITFALL
  2: a concealed explosive device contrived to go off when some harmless-looking object is touched

Source: *Merriam-Webster's Collegiate Dictionary*

For working moms, this scrambled-brain phenomenon is especially frustrating because it's exposed for all of your coworkers to see. At least at home, your baby doesn't judge you on how many times you start a sentence that you have no idea how to finish. One mom told us that she was worried about appearing forgetful at work for fear that her manager would use this to bolster his opinion that working moms were hard to manage. Your boss and coworkers remember how you were "before," and are bound to notice little changes, like the fact that you're wearing mismatched socks, or have spit-up on your shoulder. Unfortunately, they'll probably notice bigger changes too, like when you ask to have a question repeated or miss a meeting because you had to take your baby to the doctor or because you just plain spaced it. The problem isn't so much that they notice these things; it's the negative stereotype they associate with you and then extend to all working moms. And who wants to contribute to the mommy-track image we're trying so hard to overcome?

Worse than the image is the real fear that if you are unable to be alert and productive, you may get a poor performance evaluation or even lose your job. It's a vicious cycle. The more stressed you get about your work, the more frazzled you become. The more frazzled, the more likely someone will notice if your performance isn't up to par.

Here's the kicker: the symptoms are real. Studies have shown that memory loss and concentration lapses are measurable among pregnant and postpartum women. Although there's no proven link between memory loss, anxiety, and the inability to concentrate, our own unscientific research suggests that these all go hand in hand, and that raging hormones and sleep deprivation are to blame. Doctors and scientists have spent countless dollars and hours proving what we Milk Mamas already know. Prolonged sleeplessness affects our brain cells, causing memory loss. Add to this the complexity of managing a household, maintaining marital and family relationships, meeting others' needs, caring for a newborn, *and* performing well in our jobs. It's no wonder our brains feel fuzzy.

Wednesday, October 31

Happy Halloween! Here's how my day started. In the car with Sara by 7:15 A.M., feeling so proud of myself! Diaper bag √, pump √, security badge √, purse √, lunch √, laptop √, Sara √, Sara's favorite blanket √, Sara's coat and hat √√, car keys √, sunglasses √, new favorite lip gloss √.

Halfway to day care, I realized I was wearing my slippers! I raced back home, ran inside leaving Sara in the car crying (she hates her car seat). Sprinted up the stairs in time to grab ringing phone. Rudely cut off my clueless mother-in-law. By the time I hung up the phone, I couldn't remember what it was I forgot. I ran back to the car hoping it would trigger my memory. Shoes! Needless to say, I was 20 minutes late getting to work. I walked past my evil boss as he gave me a dirty look. I hate my job. I want to be with Sara, listening to her say "ah goo" all day!

Fighting back tears, Sam

Wednesday, October 31

Sam,

We've all been there. It's the worst. It's that whole sleep-deprivation torture thing. I have an idea. Let's play a Halloween trick on him. I'm thinking razor blades in apples? No, that's too mean! How about this: let's make prank phone calls to him in the middle of the night so he's as tired as we are.

Anne

Wednesday, October 31

What if he has caller ID???

I know: drop some Lunesta or Ambien into his coffee, and for God's sake—nothing but decaf!!

Stacy

Wednesday, October 31

Samantha,

Don't let Evil Boss ruin your day. Is he a dad? Surely not, or he would be more understanding. Even so, if IBM wants to live up to its family-friendly image, people like your manager are going to have to come around and accept, and even *support*, working moms. What's his problem?! Sheesh.

Cate

Thursday, November 1

Evil Boss is a working mom's nightmare: 39, single, works 70+ hour weeks, too good-looking for his own good, egomaniac, Harvard Business School alum, and drives a black Mercedes sports car with tinted windows.

Sam

Thursday, November 1

He belongs on Wall Street in wing tips, *not* in Boulder.

Anne

Thursday, November 1

Maybe some day Evil Boss will have kids of his own. A few months of colicky crying would put him in his place.

We had so many trick-or-treaters last night. They were adorable. But everytime the doorbell rang, our dog, Daisy,

284 THE MILK MEMOS

barked her head off. We turned out the lights and put Charlotte to bed at 8:00, but a whole group of teenagers (wearing baseball caps for costumes, and carrying pillowcases full of candy) rang the doorbell at 9:30!!! Of course Daisy's barking woke Charlotte up, and we couldn't get her back to sleep until after 11:00, and she woke up 3 times during the night. Here's to another hazy day at work. . . .

Cate

Friday, November 2

Me again. Notebook hog. I was thinking about how tired and forgetful we all are, and I remembered this funny story about my sister Louise. Talk about brain drain! When Louise's second child was a few months old, she drove around with expired license plates for months. Even after her husband pointed it out, she just never had time to go to the DMV and stand in line for an hour. She drove carefully and parked in odd places, hoping to avoid getting a ticket. Finally she took time off work to get the darn license plate renewed. It took forever, and she was rushing to get back to work, but she decided to take a second to put the new expiration sticker on, because it would be just her luck to get pulled over now. After putting the sticker on, she pushed the button on her key ring, but the car didn't unlock. Instead, a car in the next row chirped and flashed its lights. It was HER car in the next row! She had just put the new expiration sticker on SOMEONE ELSE'S silver car that wasn't even the same make as hers!!!

To be continued this afternoon . . .

Cate

Friday, November 2

Oh my gosh! That is *so* something I would do. LOL! Needed that, Sam

Friday, November 2

Me too!

Anne ☺

Friday, November 2

OK, so Louise was standing there by the car wondering what to do, when a guy walked up giving her this look like she must have hit his car. She explained her mistake as she quickly tried to remove the extra sticky sticker from his license plate. It came off in three pieces, but luckily didn't damage his original sticker too much. So then she had to go back into the DMV and wait in line again. She said, "I was trying to straighten my expiration sticker out, and it tore in pieces!" They gave her a new sticker without too much hassle, and she made sure to put it on her own car.

And she's the smart one in the family!

Cate

Friday, November 2

Cate,

Thanks for that great story!!

Stacy

Friday, November 2

You just gave me another great idea—I'm going to slyly remove the expiration sticker from Evil Boss's Mercedes! Ha!

Sam

HANG IN THERE

The biggest antidote to the brain-drain phenomenon is time. Before you celebrate your baby's first birthday, you'll be able to keep track of your car keys (and remember where you parked your car) in addition to managing your work. In the meantime, remember that the good days will outnumber the bad. You will have moments of clarity and even genius amidst the fog. So don't let a few mishaps get you down, or worse, become fodder for doubting coworkers and managers who are looking for reasons to label you. If you're late to a morning meeting, don't give ammunition by over-explaining, "I'm sorry! I overslept because Susie was up five times last night, and then I had to make two trips to day care because I forgot her bottles." Instead, say professionally, "Sorry I'm late. What did I miss?" Finally, give yourself a pep talk, remembering that every single person you work with is here because of his or her mom. Plus, working moms represent a sizeable chunk of the American workforce. According to the U.S. Department of Labor, more than 25 million mothers (with children under eighteen years of age) are in the workforce, accounting for almost 20 percent of the employed population. Considering this (not to mention all the stellar qualities of working moms, described below), they couldn't exactly get by without us!

HABITS OF HIGHLY EFFECTIVE MOMS

In time, many Milk Mamas actually find themselves becoming more focused and therefore more productive and successful in their work. Working moms are unlikely to waste much time standing around the proverbial water cooler dishing up office gossip, or discussing the upcoming sale at Macy's. It's not that we become antisocial, it's just that we put a higher priority on time management. We are übermotivated to finish our work by 5:00 P.M. so that we can get home to be with our babies. One Mama, an executive at a publishing company, reduced her workday by two hours after her daughter was born, but accomplished as much in nine hours as she used to in eleven. She now eats lunch at her desk, leaves things unfinished at the end of the day, and occasionally wraps up a few things after her daughter goes to bed for the night.

Beyond time management, moms tend to streamline and weed out tasks that are extraneous. A university professor explained that after having her son, she focused clearly on what she knew would make her successful, and then devised a strategy to make it happen in the time available without shortchanging her son. She learned to delegate more effectively and became more selective in how she invested her time. She didn't let motherhood slow her path to achieving tenure.

Motherhood brings out many qualities that make star employees and leaders. Moms tend to be patient, flexible, understanding, and natural communicators, skilled at multitasking, planning, pushing back, setting limits, and dealing with chaos and shades of gray. And truly, any mom who has convinced a screaming child to get out of the pool and go home for a nap, or simply to get in her car seat, has learned the art of negotiation.

SOMETHING'S GOTTA GIVE

Despite the virtues and added value that working mothers bring, the reality is that many employers still perceive moms negatively. Working moms are viewed as less willing to work long hours, travel, or shift their schedules to accommodate emergencies. And let's face it, many of us *are* less willing to make the same sacrifices we did before having children. One Mama, a senior solutions architect for a small technology services company, said there's no doubt that the way she was perceived—*and* her own aspirations—changed dramatically the second she found out she was pregnant. Before having her daughter, she was a perfectionist on the fast track, taking on more work than she needed to and eagerly traveling and hobnobbing with clients from coast to coast. Afterward, her colleagues and clients saw her in a whole different way, and with good reason. She acknowledges that she's become more of a reactive problem solver than a go-getter who travels at the drop of a hat, constantly creating and jumping at new opportunities. These days, she finds herself doing a good job rather than an outstanding one . . . and she's OK with that for the first time in her life.

Certainly, there are moms out there who don't skip a beat in their careers after having children. The moms we know whose careers are seemingly unchanged by having children are the primary breadwinners in their families and have an intricate web of support systems, from housekeepers, full-time nannies, "errand elves," and even personal chefs to husbands who temper their own career ambitions to take on substantial parenting or take the leap to become stay-at-home dads.

All working parents pay a price. We either put less emphasis on our careers in favor of our children or we spend less time with our children (making sure they're well cared for, of course) in order to keep our careers charging ahead. Make peace with whatever price you choose to pay, knowing that the right balance between work and family is different for everyone. The degree of peace you achieve will depend upon what truly feeds your soul the most (career, motherhood, or just the right combination), and the amount of flexibility and support you have.

THE MOTHERHOOD PENALTY

While employers won't openly admit a bias against working moms, there's enough anecdotal evidence to prove that it exists. And it's not exactly subtle. One Milk Mama who worked for a multinational, high-tech corporation was afraid to tell her manager she was pregnant. When she finally did, her manager slammed the door in her face, and wouldn't talk to her for the rest of the day. We read about a female sales manager whose boss told her (in front of her all-male colleagues) that she could put her birth control pills on the expense account, because getting pregnant would be the worst thing she could do to the team. Another Mama delayed telling her boss about her pregnancy until she received her promotion—just in time, as the safety pins and rubber bands holding her slacks together were reaching their limit.

Shelly Correll, associate professor at Cornell University, tested the theory of a Motherhood Penalty by sending nearly identical fictitious résumés to a communications company. Some of the résumés mentioned that the applicant was active in the Parent-Teacher Association. The PTA applicants were 44 percent less likely to be considered for the job.

To overcome this penalty, we need to change the workplace mindset. As it is, the childless worker who stays at the office until 8:00 P.M. is often seen as the more committed employee, even if she's surfing the Net. On the flip side, the working parent is often criticized for leaving at 5:00 P.M. on the dot and taking time off for everything from doctor's appointments to track meets, even if she's a star performer. The nonmother resents it if she's left to take up the slack; the mom gets angry if she's unfairly labeled a slacker. Even more bitter is the part-time mom who works her tail off but isn't viewed as serious, loyal, or promotable. These tensions escalate office politics to a new level, making it even more difficult for moms (and others) to enjoy their jobs and feel valued for the positive qualities they bring. The new benchmark for A-team employees shouldn't have to do with face time, an 8:00 A.M.–to–5:00 P.M. schedule, or parental status. Instead, results, quality of work, dependability, and attitude of the employee should be the litmus tests.

HEADS HELD HIGH

Even though it seems the deck is stacked against us, we must constantly remind ourselves and other Mamas of our value. The skills and strengths we possessed prior to motherhood are still there! Sure, there's an initial period of sleep deprivation, "mommy brain," and adjustment to having a baby. But along with that come maternal qualities that can actually improve results and, at the same time, create a positive, more desirable work environment. In fact, a recent study by WorldWIT, a network for women in business and technology, found that 69 percent of employees would rather work for a mother than a nonmother because they find mothers to be better listeners and more understanding of family demands.

Only you can decide whether now is the time to excel in your career. Many women blossom in their careers once they become moms. A literary agent Mama said that since having her son, she has cut her work schedule by 25 percent but has more than doubled her sales. She attributes her success to experience as well as her maniacal insistence on prioritization. She doesn't take anything on unless she really cares about it and believes it has huge potential. After surviving childbirth and the slings and arrows of taking care of a newborn, she feels much more confident and believes she can tackle anything, talk to anyone, and get anything done. Nothing scares her.

Even though we shouldn't have to prove our worth all over again at work once we become mothers (fathers don't), the fact is, we do. Keeping this in mind, go back to work with your eyes open and head held high. Don't tolerate negative comments about the length of your maternity leave, the flexible hours you work, or your reluctance to travel. By remaining confident and determined, we can use our motherhood moxie to prove the naysayers wrong!

. . .

SIXTEEN

detour ahead

Monday, November 5

Good morning! Hope everyone had a good weekend. We did! But now that I'm back at work, it all feels like a distant memory. Brought in a *People* magazine so we can catch up on celebrity breakups and makeups.

Sam

SHIT! My pump just stopped working and won't turn back on. I don't know what's wrong with this thing, and I'm only halfway done! What now? Crap. I'll have to ask Evil Boss if I can leave early to nurse Sara and figure out how to fix my pump.

Monday, November 5

Sam,

Good Grief! Are you Charlie Brown? When I first came back to work, I was jinxed, too, not to mention clueless. If you look back in the notebook, you can read all about the soap explosion in my pump bag and the time I melted all my pump parts on the stove. I started with a Barbie pump (might as well have been), which broke. And look at me now—Most Improved Milk Mama. You're next.

Andrea

Monday, November 5

Sam,

If your pump is still on the fritz—and if this doesn't give you the creeps—you're welcome to borrow my pump. Just hook up your tubing and parts and squirt away!

Cate

Monday, November 5

Sorry to hear about the pump crisis! Thanks for the *People* magazine. Since when has Michael Jackson been white? Just kidding . . . I'm not *that* out of it!

Anne

Monday, November 5

Sam,

Did you buy your pump new? If so, take it back to the store. I'm sure it's under warranty. If you borrowed, maybe the motor just pooped out. They don't last forever. Depending on how long you think you'll keep pumping, you could look into renting one instead of forking out $200.

Stacy

Tuesday, November 6

Are you ready for this?

I QUIT! I gave my two-week notice yesterday. EB hit a new low. When I called to tell him I needed to leave early yesterday, he got very short with me and said I could go only after I finished booking his travel plans to Europe. I started to tell him I could easily do that later from home, when he actually HUNG UP on me! Can you believe it?! I called him right back and told him I couldn't do this anymore. I'm still in shock, but think it's the right thing. My last day will be the 16th.

Sam

P.S. My pump had a bad adapter. I got a new one and am now back in business (with my pump anyway).

Tuesday, November 6

What an ass! If your family can get by without your income, I say go for it. I know I would. You go girl,

Anne

Tuesday, November 6

WOW—big decision you made, and I applaud you for it. Above all, you must be true to your values, yourself, and Sara. What was EB's reaction?

Cate

Tuesday, November 6

Have you ruled out getting a different job in IBM or working for a different manager? Not everyone is like EB and I think you'd have a much better experience working for an actual human. All my managers at IBM have been pretty darn understanding and supportive. You could also try to find something more flexible, like working from home, part-time, or job share. I'll keep my fingers crossed!

Stacy

Tuesday, November 6

After the adrenaline wore off, I thought about whether I should have kept my cool and made a more graceful exit.

But deep down, I'm done with it, and I've actually been thinking about quitting for the past month. My husband, Mark, had been encouraging me to quit. He's a real estate agent, so his income can be feast or famine, but the trend is in the right direction. We both know that he has incredible potential, and he is so driven. I, on the other hand, am a fish out of water at IBM, and I'm just plain miserable. I guess it was only a matter of time before I snapped, so why prolong working when I don't have to and I can't stand it? You know how it is—every day I miss with Sara I'll never get back. Our family will have to make some major adjustments . . . maybe even move to a smaller house. But it's worth it to us.

As far as EB goes, he was definitely surprised, and actually speechless (for two seconds anyway). Then the robot kicked in, and said, "Well, I'm sorry that you couldn't make it work. Please go ahead and begin documenting your desk procedures. I'd like to get someone else on board quickly so we don't miss a beat."

Sam

Tuesday, November 6

I echo Anne: what an ass!

Andrea

ONE BAD EGG

Even the best companies have bad managers. It's hard enough making the transition back to work without being mistreated by someone who is insensitive and unable to adapt to the new you. Managers and coworkers can be unsupportive for a variety of reasons. Sure, there are jerks out there, but there are also good people who just can't get their heads around your family-centered priorities. Some managers can't let go of their power and control, and in their stubbornness, won't accommodate your needs. Some managers are jealous of you because they regret the time they dedicated to work when their children were young. If they don't have children, maybe they wish they did. Or some are single and never learned work-life balance. Their work habits have become so ingrained that they have lost sight of life beyond their laptops, and their isolation becomes painfully evident when they see how you juggle the needs of your family. In the end, the inflexibility is really more about your boss or coworker than it is about you. That's little consolation if you have to work with a nimrod after maternity leave. But if you don't take it personally, it's easier to concentrate on your job, still enjoy time with your family, and not get so rattled by nasty remarks or dirty looks.

ONE BRAVE SOUL

Unfortunately, people who rigidly hold on to the way things have always been done are creating a work environment that looks nothing like the utopia we read about in "100 Best Companies for Working Moms" or "Flexibility at Work" articles. Although it seems every company is eager to promote flexible work options and family-friendly policies, too often the reality doesn't live up to the words.

The workplace plods along because cultural change depends upon individual behavior. Since we can't change our bosses or coworkers, we must start by changing ourselves. When you notice that actions don't match words, call it out. Be the squeaky wheel. The reason we no longer hear racial jokes or tolerate sexual harassment in the office is that many courageous individuals finally said, "Enough." Fundamentally, everyone in the workplace, including mothers, is entitled to be treated with dignity and respect.

At a bare minimum, you have the right to take whatever time you need to pump breastmilk during the workday. Twelve progressive states have enacted legislation to enforce this. You also have the right to participate in the flexible work programs offered by your company without being subjected to gossip, snide remarks, and exasperated sighs.

Sure, we have to meet the needs of the business. But too frequently the needs of the business serve as a convenient excuse for ignoring the needs of the individual. There is certainly room to meet both. Do not accept a workplace that marginalizes working moms or creates a culture of hypocrisy, where HR spouts family-friendly policies and practices but doesn't actually deliver.

The next time you hear, "There's no room on my staff for a part-time person. . . . The client won't be comfortable with a job share. . . . We need you at your desk from 8:00 A.M. to 5:00 P.M. every day. . . . Your (part-time) performance doesn't compare favorably to your (full-time) peers," raise a flag. While your manager probably has the final say when it comes to your job, you also have some leverage, especially if you can build a case to show how your work can be done in part-time or nonconventional hours (for more on this see the Negotiation Tips box on page 310–11). No company wants to build a reputation that screams, "We don't support working moms."

Of course, if you feel you are being harassed or discriminated against, document it, professionally and privately confront the person, and if it persists, go straight to HR or upper management. Your first instinct may be to split the scene, either by quitting or transferring to a different department. This may solve the matter for you, but doing so perpetuates the problem for the next working mom. Besides, why should you have to go through the disruption and stress of moving out when you're not the culprit? The business has a responsibility to address and correct the negative behavior, even if that means moving the perpetrator out. Whether you face a colleague who rolls her eyes when you can't stay late or a manager who is downright harassing you, stand up for yourself. Don't feel one bit afraid, embarrassed, or guilty. It starts with one person taking another to task. Collectively, we'll force progress.

 know your rights

If you feel that your employer is discriminating against you because of your status as a mother or pregnant person, despite your efforts to confront and correct the situation, speak with an attorney. You have rights. (See page 5–6.) Many moms have taken their cases to court and won. While we don't advocate litigation as the solution, sometimes the only way to get an employer's attention is by hitting them where it hurts—their bottom line.

Wednesday, November 7

Sam,

I still can't believe you actually quit! I've often dreamed of walking in and quitting on the spot, just throwing my IBM badge on my manager's desk (of course, when there's a deadline looming), and leaving everything behind except the pictures of the kids. Cheerio! Off to the British Virgin Islands, lottery check in hand.

Before you go, you really should report EB through the Speak Up or Open Door process so he doesn't give IBM a bad name or make the next working mom miserable.

We'll miss you! Please leave some photos of you and Sara . . . so we can picture you doing what you love best!

Andrea

Wednesday, November 7

Here is what your desk procedures should say: "All work and no play is how Evil Boss likes his day. Sara and Sam would much rather play, even though it doesn't pay." Fill a whole binder with that! And I agree with Andrea that you need to blow the whistle on this guy. Schedule a meeting with his manager and professionally explain the situation.

> Maybe it will help the person who comes next . . . and it will also give you a sense of closure.
>
> Cate

POOPED OUT, NEED PAMPERING

Even if you enjoy your work, have a supportive manager, a healthy baby, and a happy family, don't be surprised if you still feel like quitting your job. Between six and twelve months after having a baby, you may begin to feel like you are falling apart. You worry that you can't handle one more task or unexpected event. The slightest bump in the road sends you into a tailspin. There's a reason for this: in the midst of holding down a job, managing household responsibilities, and tending to everyone else's needs, you've probably forgotten to take care of yourself. Everyone—baby or no baby—needs time to herself. Take a break. Get some exercise or just take a bath. Schedule a haircut, manicure, or massage. Spend fifteen minutes reading a chapter of a book (this one counts). Meditate. Pray. Be silent. Heck, lock yourself in the bathroom with a good magazine. And don't just do this when you're mad at your husband or PMS-ing. Plan time for yourself each day, even if it's only ten minutes. Once you've mastered this, schedule time at least monthly when you can get away for a few hours. Go on a date with your husband (remember him?) or out to dinner with your girlfriends (remember them?).

Single moms, you can do this, too. It will be harder for you to carve out your own time, but it's even more critical. Your ten minutes may be every night after the kids go to bed, or in the morning before they wake up. Or take time during the workday—a quick walk for some fresh air; a disconnected, silent lunch break; or a pumping session with relaxing music and your favorite magazine. Your budget may be tight, but it's worth eating Ramen noodles occasionally so you can pay a babysitter and get out once or twice a month. Or trade time with another mom so you can take turns going out.

Besides forgetting yourself amidst the hubbub, another factor that may be driving you to the brink of insanity is the sheer magnitude of things that need to be done, and the lack of time you have in which to do them. You can lighten the load by prioritizing and delegating at home, just as you do at work. Write down your big, ugly to-do list and start sorting and slashing. Determine what you can reasonably handle (be realistic!), what you can ask others to do for you (think husband, babysitter, older children, lawn-care service, house-keeper), and what you're not going to do at all (the scrap-book can wait). Put "time for me" at the top of the list.

Making a list, scheduling time for yourself, and lining up

babysitters and other hired help may feel like more work, but do it. It's OK to occasionally put yourself, instead of your baby, at the center of your universe. If you don't, it's only a matter of time before you reach the breaking point. Constantly remind yourself that if you're not thriving, your family won't either. After a while, you'll find yourself looking forward to (and imagining what you'll do during) the free time you've created.

PATTY-CAKE MOM
VERSUS CAREER MOM

When you've reached your limit, in spite of all efforts to maintain sanity, you may find yourself in the middle of a heated internal debate about your decision to work. (This assumes that you have the luxury of choice.) One side of you asks, *What about the years I've spent getting an advanced degree or building my career, reputation, professional network, practice, and skills? Am I ready to walk away from that to change diapers and do laundry? Will I go stir-crazy? Can I live with the title of stay-at-home mom or homemaker? Should I relinquish my financial independence? How much will our lifestyle have to change without my income? What will happen when I'm ready to go back?* The other side argues, *Motherhood is the most important, influential, challenging, and rewarding job on earth. My career can wait, but my baby cannot. The years from zero to three form the basis for my child's emotional and developmental well-being. When the timing is right, I'll go back to work. I won't pick up right where I left off, but I won't be starting from scratch either. Worst case, it will take five years to rebuild my career and income, but I'll never regret the time I spent with my baby.* And there you are, caught in the middle. Listen to both sides and research all of your options, knowing that the choice you make doesn't have to be black or white . . . and is not irreversible.

FLEXIBLE WORK OPTIONS

As with all worthy and challenging endeavors, it takes time to craft a working arrangement that enables you to feel satisfied in your job *and* in your role as a mom. Be creative!

Extended maternity leave—If you haven't yet returned to work, you could consider taking an extended leave-of-absence beyond the standard maternity leave. This is dependent upon your employer's willingness to get by without you and hold your job open for months. Or if your job is filled, you would have to be willing to undertake a job search at the end of your leave. This option also requires another source of income or a healthy savings account. Extending your leave means you get to be with your baby during the precious early months when she needs you the most. Caution: the longer you're away from work, the harder it may be to return. You will probably feel "out of shape" workwise, and unenthusiastic about going back to the pace and structure of work.

Working from home—If your job is conducive to it, try working from home. Whether you do this occasionally, a couple days a week, or every day, you may find that the additional time with your baby eases the work-versus-motherhood conflict. Instead of spending time getting ready for work in the morning and commuting, you can enjoy extra time hugging, tickling, and nursing your baby. For more on working from home, see Chapter 12.

Part-time—If it's financially feasible, and depending on your line of work, you could go part-time. The challenge is rescoping a full-time job into part-time hours. This requires eliminating work or finding another person to take on that work. If you don't have a good plan for how the "extra" work will get done, chances are you'll end up trying to do all the work yourself, putting in full time and effort yet being paid for less, and getting stressed out and resentful in the process. Your success and satisfaction with a part-time job depend primarily upon your ability to contain the job to your new working hours.

Job sharing—A more recent twist on part-time schedules is job sharing, where two workers share the duties of one full-time job. If you're interested in job sharing and your employer is supportive, the ideal approach is to begin planning well before your maternity leave begins. Finding a compatible work partner is key. Look for someone who wants to work part-time, has matching or complementary skills, a similar work style, and who connects and communicates with you well. The trick to making a job share work is showing that the two of you are interchangeable and are just as efficient as one person (or more so).

Flextime—A popular option in many companies is to customize your work schedule according to your needs and preferences. This could mean working shortened hours during the day and completing the remaining hours in the evening, after putting your baby to sleep. Your work hours could vary by day, depending on your family needs. Many parents take advantage of flextime by staggering their workdays. For example, one parent works from 6:30 A.M. to 3:30 P.M., and the other works from 9:00 A.M. to 6:00 P.M. They divide and conquer school or day-care drop-offs, after-school activities, and cooking dinner.

Compressed workweek—A variation on flextime is to remain full-time, but to complete your work in a compressed schedule. For example, you could work four ten-hour days followed by three days off, or three twelve-hour days followed by four days off. Of course, the hard part is the long separations from your baby, especially if you're breastfeeding—you'll have to pump three or four times while at work. The good news is that it's like having a long weekend every ~~week~~, with more full days to be with your baby.

 negotiation tips

Once you know which work option you want, prepare a rock-solid proposal to convince your employer. Don't pop the question during a casual conversation in the bathroom, hallway, elevator, or parking lot. Instead, prepare a written proposal, which should include a clear definition of the work arrangement you want, your commitment to and plan for completing your work, success stories (if you have them), and benefits to you and your employer. Benefits for your employer could include:

- *Retention*—Your skill set and experience are valuable. By retaining you, your manager will avoid recruiting and training costs.
- *Productivity*—Research shows that people tend to go the extra mile for businesses that offer flexible options.
- *Morale*—When employees' needs are met, their satisfaction rubs off on coworkers and promotes a positive culture. This also attracts prospective new talent.

- *Reduced salary costs*—In an environment where cost cutting is paramount, your employer may jump at the chance to save a portion of your salary.

Don't be surprised if the first answer is no. You might propose a trial period of a few weeks, during which you can prove that the arrangement you want works fine. Many of the Mamas we know succeeded in getting the flexible work arrangement they needed only after negotiating for months, and finally threatening to quit. We don't suggest starting with an ultimatum, but you may end up there, and it just may work.

Downshift—You could make a conscious decision to slow down at work, relaxing your career ambitions and relieving the pressure (self-imposed and external) to constantly achieve. This doesn't mean you become a slacker; it just means that you say no more often, finish the Important Project tomorrow, and stop at "good enough." Or you could consider making a more overt change in your work pace. One Mama, a mother of two, and a partner in her law firm for seven years, decided to give up her partnership and take on less litigation work in order to spend more time with her kids. Another attorney sacrificed the partner track at a prestigious firm but kept alive her ultimate goal of becoming a law school professor. A software engineer Mama with two small children asked for a demotion and to be taken off the company's executive resource list. All of these moms described their decisions as wrenching, but also liberating.

Lane change—None of these appeal? Consider transitioning to a career that is geared to independence and flexibility. An entire industry has emerged from the Tupperware parties of old. Today women, mostly moms, start their own businesses selling everything from kitchen utensils to sex toys at in-home parties on evenings or weekends. In fact, according to the National Association of Women Business Owners, there are more than 10 million female-owned businesses in the United States. Work-at-home moms even have their own acronym—WAHMs—and do everything from freelance work in writing, editing, Web design, graphic design, desktop publishing, or consulting, to massage, pet care, tutoring, in-home day care, cleaning, landscaping, or catering. You could even become a personal shopper, organizer, scrapbooker, or . . . how about a doula or lactaction consultant!

Pit crew—If your family can get by on just one income, and yours is the higher of the two, perhaps your husband could become a stay-at-home dad. For this to work, you both need to be truly satisfied in your roles—as a breadwinner, and as a full-time father. And you both have to keep jealousy in check. One Mama, an HR director at a major resort, raves about her stay-at-home husband. She readily admits that he is better suited to be a full-time parent—he is more outgoing, scheduled, and play oriented, and better at discipline. He takes care of everything from running errands and grocery shopping to driving thirty miles to swim lessons . . . and he's even organized his own play group. The arrangement works fabulously for both parents. She is filled with gratitude and pride, and wouldn't want it any other way, but that doesn't mean it's easy. It tugs at her heart when their girls wake up saying "Daddy!" or run to him to kiss an owie. Although being a stay-at-home parent of two is intense, this father feels his life has true purpose now, and is glad to be raising adventurous daughters who can walk barefoot on pebbles or hike in the snow.

This brings up one more key to success. Dads inevitably have a different style from moms, and you have to learn to accept—and even appreciate—the differences. One Mama of two gave her husband explicit instructions for his first day as a stay-at-home dad. She wrote down a schedule and packed a bag complete with snacks, lunch, toys, spare outfits, diapers (regular and swimming), floaties, towels, sunscreen, wipes, and a first-aid kit. Her husband called several times throughout the day to assure her that everything was going great. When she got home from work, both kids were happily eating popsicles and playing in the backyard, unphased by the fact that they were still wearing the regular diapers that they'd gone swimming in. The diapers were poofy and sagging down to their knees, still dripping with pool water. This Mama felt like firing her husband on the spot, but then realized that her kids were just fine and that it was OK for them to find their own groove with Dad.

Off ramp—There is one more option (for some moms): *you* could be the one who takes on one of the toughest and most important jobs in the world by becoming a stay-at-home mom. Giving up paid work means making cutbacks and walking away (temporarily at least) from a career you've built. One Mama, a print production manager for a major financial services company, decided to call it quits eight months after returning from maternity leave, leaving behind a career path she'd built over thirteen years. She liked the company and the people, but not the pace or pressure. Although the transition to full-time stay-at-home mom was difficult at first, she hasn't looked back and doesn't miss work in the least. She used to wonder what "those stay-at-home moms" did all day, but now knows that her days at home are just as busy as, if not busier than, the days she was at work. At least when she was working, she could start her day by reading the paper, enjoying a cup of coffee, and then listening to National Public Radio on her way to work. When she became a stay-at-home mom, she had to be "ON" from the moment her baby woke her up wanting breastmilk. No more easing into her day. Now, her boss was in her face demanding attention before she had even gotten out of bed and used the bathroom. Like the vast majority of working moms who exit the workforce, she doesn't plan to return to the company she left. Many Mamas opt not to return to work at all, or seek the flexibility of smaller companies. Some start their own businesses, and most don't return to full-time jobs. Though they lose significant earning power, in return they've gained irreplaceable time with their little ones, and vice versa. This may be worth all the paychecks and promotions in the world.

Friday, November 16

Here it is. My last day. It still hasn't sunk in. Maybe it will feel real when I wake up Monday morning and realize that I don't have to rush Sara to day care. I'll get to hug her all day long!

The thing I'll miss most about IBM is the people. Especially you Milk Mamas. Thank you so much for all your help this past month. I couldn't have survived without you. I wish you all—and your babies and families—the very best!

Moo! Sam

P.S. Can I still be in the Club?

Friday, November 16

Sam,

We will miss you too!!! We're so happy for you. Enjoy every minute (try, anyway). Don't worry, your membership in the Milk Mama Club is good for a lifetime! Send us an e-mail every now and then to let us know how you're doing. Include pics of Sara!

Love, Cate

• • •

the graduate

Monday, November 19

Happy Turkey week everyone! Let's hear it for a short workweek! Ella, Ryan, and I are going to have Thanksgiving dinner at a friend's house. I offered to bring the rice cereal, pureed bananas, and breastmilk since that's the only thing Ryan will eat.

Anne

Monday, November 19

Gobble gobble! Anne, bananas on Thanksgiving??? Ryan needs to try sweet potatoes! My little Charlotte will get her first taste of birthday cake—she turns 1 on Thanksgiving Day!

☺☹ Cate

(We think Charlotte's high chair is sticky and yucky now—here comes frosting!)

Monday, November 19

No! Charlotte can't be 1 already! But what a perfect thing to celebrate on Thanksgiving.

We're going to serve Caleb his FAVORITE: Gerber turkey sticks with the skins cut off. Yum!

Andrea

Monday, November 19

What's with those turkey sticks? I think they're actually Vienna sausages in a Gerber jar! And the smell—P.U.!

My grandparents are flying in from Florida tonight—bless their hearts for braving the crowds and the cold. While I'm cooking the turkey, I'll put Grandma to work knitting me a breastpump cozy. Lord knows she's already knitted everything else under the sun. The boys have at least 3 of everything—blankets, hats, sweaters, mittens, and even scarves (those went straight to storage when Colby nearly strangled George). I swear she would knit diapers if she could.

Stacy

Tuesday, November 20

Oooooh! I want a breastpump cozy, too. Baby blue, please!

Anne

Tuesday, November 20

When your grandma's done knitting cozies, maybe she could knit a shawl for all of us Milk Mamas to use when we pump. Brrrrrrrrr!

Andrea

Tuesday, November 20

How is Grandma at speed knitting? Charlotte would love a pink sweater for her 1st birthday. I can't believe it's in 2 days! How can it be?? I'm afraid the next time I blink, she'll be heading out to the prom in a strapless dress, heels, and a wrist corsage. With Caleb as her date, *of course*.

Cate

Tuesday, November 20

Cate,

What color will Charlotte's prom dress be? (So I can rent Caleb's tux with matching cumberbund. What a funny word that is—cumberbund cumberbund cumberbund.)

Are you going to wean Charlotte? You can't leave us!

Andrea

Tuesday, November 20

I'm totally in denial about Charlotte's birthday. I want her to *always* be my baby.

My pediatrician is encouraging me to transition to cow's milk, breastfeeding just at night and maybe in the morning. I should be relieved to give up pumping, but instead I feel sad. Pumping still seems like the most meaningful thing I do during the day. On the other hand, we're still trying to get pregnant and I wonder if we'll have better luck when I wean. I don't want to wait two years to get pregnant again!

Cate

P.S. I'm taking tomorrow off. My parents are in town for Thanksgiving and Charlotte's birthday. Happy Thanksgiving, everyone!!

Tuesday, November 20

First of all, don't listen to your pediatrician! Second, it's still possible to get prego while breastfeeding. So, I say breastfeed as long as you want. I give you credit for wanting to keep it up. As for me, I'm counting the days until I can give my breastpump the heave-ho. One year is plenty.

Stacy

P.S. Happy birthday, Charlotte! Congratulations, Cate, on nursing for a full year!! I always knew you could do it.

Wednesday, November 21
Ditto!
Anne
Wednesday, November 21
Happy Birthday, Charlotte! I want to hear all about the cake mess.
Happy Thanksgiving, you guys!
Andrea

WHEN TO WEAN

There will be a last time you nurse your baby. Whether you're looking forward to having your breasts back to yourself, perhaps indulging in more than a "celebratory single, small alcoholic drink," or you're dreading the day your baby no longer cuddles close and suckles at your breast, weaning is another step in the motherly process of letting go. Separation starts when the doctor (or your nervous husband) cuts your baby's umbilical cord, ending nine (okay, ten) months of unity in which you and your baby were completely intertwined. From then on, it continues in gradual steps: your baby begins sleeping in her own room rather than yours, eating sweet potatoes and pureed bananas in addition to your breastmilk, waving good-bye to you at day care, wiggling to get out of your arms and go explore, crawling, then walking, then running away from you, and learning the word "no!" It's an endless process, but thank God it doesn't happen all at once.

As with all baby milestones, there is no right time to wean. Some babies naturally lose interest in nursing, some reach a point when they can take it or leave it, and others are nursing fanatics. The same is true for mothers. Your baby's cues and your own feelings and needs should be your guides as you decide when to wean. Ideally, you and your baby will be on the same page. However, it is more likely that you will be ready to wean before your baby is.

We know plenty of Mamas who reach their limit when it comes to nursing in the middle of the night, or find that nursing depletes their energy and (because they're too drained or have no time to exercise) prevents them from getting back into shape. And what working Mama doesn't get tired of lugging a pump around, finding a place and time to pump, washing parts, and transporting milk? Only you can decide if any of these reasons is enough to convince you to wean. Keep in mind that it doesn't have to be all or nothing. You could continue nursing but slowly wean from pumping, substituting formula (or cow's milk for babies over twelve months) during the day. Or you could decide to nurse less, keeping only the one or two nursing times you treasure most and having your partner supplement with formula when you're at aerobics class or sound asleep.

Many Mamas first consider weaning when they are ready to get pregnant again because they fear that breastfeeding will reduce their odds of conceiving. During the first six months (when you probably don't want to get pregnant anyway!), breastfeeding can greatly reduce your chances of becoming pregnant because the breastmilk-producing hormone prolactin prevents your ovaries from releasing eggs. But beware: it's not a foolproof method of contraception, especially if you're not nursing frequently and exclusively. Once your period has returned and your baby is older than six months, you're back in the game. While still breastfeeding, you can increase your chances of getting pregnant by shortening each feeding, and encouraging more time between feedings, making sure you have at least one six-hour period without breastfeeding during the day (or night).

While there are a myriad of perfectly legitimate reasons to wean, there are also common misconceptions that could cause you to wean prematurely. First of all, you don't need to wean your baby because she's sprouting teeth. Biting is uncommon and can easily be corrected. (See pages 187–89 for more information on biting.) Also, if you have a baby who refuses solids, don't reduce or eliminate nursing as a way to encourage him to devour a jar of peas. Breastmilk is the most important source of nutrition throughout a baby's first year. Weaning would only deprive your baby of the nutrition he needs most. Also, don't be tempted to wean to make your baby less clingy. Your little one naturally craves closeness with you, and weaning may only make him more of a Velcro baby.

And for goodness' sake, don't let societal mores dictate your weaning timeline. We all know that the older a baby gets, especially beyond a year, the more societal pressure there is to wean. Although a stranger may smile at you as you nurse your six-week-old infant on a park bench, that same stranger will likely scowl if you nurse your eighteen-month-old toddler in a public place. Moms who decide to breastfeed past a year often turn into closet nursers, not admitting their secret nursing habit even to close friends, coworkers, or relatives. But these moms shouldn't have to hide. There's good evidence that breastmilk continues to have immunological benefits well into the second year and beyond, never mind the emotional and nutritional advantages. Consider the fact that worldwide, on average, children don't wean until they are two to four years old!

recommended breastfeeding duration

The American Academy of Pediatrics recommends exclusive breastfeeding for approximately the first six months and supports breastfeeding for the first year and beyond *as long as mutually desired by mother and child*.

Source: American Academy of Pediatrics Policy Statement on Breastfeeding, February 2005.

DON'T QUIT COLD TURKEY

Once you've decided when to wean, plan a slow approach. Just as your nursing relationship developed gradually, so should weaning. For many babies, nursing is the ultimate security blanket, calming and soothing them like nothing else. Yanking this away would be traumatic for both of you. Besides, stopping suddenly can cause engorgement, plugged ducts, mastitis, and even depression. Allow plenty of time for weaning, so your hormone levels and milk production can slowly taper. Actually, you'll be amazed how long it takes for your breasts to stop producing milk, especially after all the time you've spent worrying about making enough milk. One Milk Mama let her son try nursing a month after weaning to prove to him that the milk was all gone. Imagine her surprise (and her son's delight) when the milk started flowing again. Because Mother Nature is determined to make sure your baby doesn't go hungry, it can take two to four months for the well to run dry. While your body is transitioning slowly during the weaning process, you and your baby will have time to adjust to the loss of nursing time—those quiet, intimate moments that were a necessary part of your daily routine.

WEANING GRACEFULLY

When you're ready to wean, here are some ideas to ease the transition for you and your baby:

- *Give up one nursing session at a time.* Save your favorite one for last. You might start by giving up the morning nursing first, followed by the "mommy's home from work" nursing, and finally, the bedtime nursing. Allow at least three to four weeks for weaning, subtracting no more than one nursing time per week, until your baby doesn't nurse at all. However, if this feels too quick for you, be flexible—there's no rush.

- *Express only enough milk as needed to relieve discomfort.* Dropping one feeding at a time should minimize the risk of engorgement, but as you taper, you may experience some uncomfortable fullness.
- *Give cabbage leaves a try.* It sounds like an old wives' tale, but placing cold cabbage leaves inside your bra really can make you more comfortable. Likewise, placing cold gel or ice packs (brrrr!) against your breasts can help reduce swelling. It's not a career booster to have cabbage leaves or ice packs peeking out from your V-neck sweater while at work, so these techniques are best tried at home.
- *Anticipate your child's hunger.* Don't wait until he's screaming and can only be soothed by breastmilk. For older babies, keep snacks on hand and offer a bottle or cup of milk as a substitute.
- *Don't bind your breasts!* This is an outdated and unnecessarily painful practice which should go the way of corsets and granny girdles. Binding can cause plugged ducts or worse. Instead, wear a supportive cotton bra, like a sports bra, that is snug but not uncomfortable.
- *Substitute a new activity in place of nursing.* This could be anything from giving a bottle in bed while snuggling together in the morning to walking the dog around the block after work or reading an extra book at bedtime.

- *Be generous with your time and affection.* When you give up nursing, your baby still craves alone time and hugs and kisses from you. Reassure her that you're still there for her even though your breasts aren't.
- *Involve your partner.* When you give up your bedtime nursing, it might be easiest if your husband puts your baby to sleep. When you stop nursing in the morning, he can wake your baby up with a big smile and warm bottle of milk.

Monday, November 26

Thanks for all the happy-birthday wishes. Charlotte's 1st birthday was wonderful. I think it should *always* be a national holiday. We slept in (yea!), and even took a bath together in the morning—one of our favorite things. I was telling my girlfriend all about it as we were walking to the cafeteria for coffee. We passed a group of people just as I said, "We had a nice bubble bath together—it was so great!" So they heard that totally out of context. I thought: oh good! Let them think that my husband and I are actually still that romantic.

Cate

Monday, November 26

That is so funny! But really, if you're trying to have another baby, a romantic bubble bath with Chris isn't such a bad idea!

Andrea

Monday, November 26

Romance and bubble bath? What are you talking about?

Anne

Tuesday, November 27

As I reflect on the past year, one of the things I'm most proud of is that Miss Charlotte Ellen Smith has not consumed *one single drop* of formula. Breastmilk all the way, baby! Wonder if I can include that in my performance review?

I think the biggest reason I'm cuckoo for breastfeeding is that, in terms of intimacy and pure motherhood, it's the next best thing to being pregnant. I'm not ready to wean, but when I do, I know I'll miss it like crazy. Believe it or not, I'm even going to miss pumping. But I've decided that in the next few weeks, I'm going to wean Mrs. Beasley (my pump!), but not Charlotte. Keep your fingers crossed that Mr. Stork won't overlook me.

Cate

Tuesday, November 27

Cate,

You are an inspiration. Even after you wean Mrs. B., you have to drop in now and then to say hi, cheer us on, update us on Charlotte's newest accomplishments, and let us know when you're PG!

I want to thank you. You're a big part of the reason I made it this long nursing Caleb. I never thought I'd grow to love nursing this much, especially since I had such a rough start. I'll always be grateful to you and all the Milk Mamas in this room!

XOXO, Andrea

P.S. I can't believe I'm getting all misty-eyed about pumping!

Tuesday, November 27

Cate,

Don't forget to post Charlotte's picture to the Graduate Wall, right next to Colby and Sara. George will be next—only a little over a month to go for us and them I'm bronzing Sally the Suckinator for posterity.

Time to start recruiting more Milk Mamas!

Stacy

EIGHTEEN

• • •

big news!

Hi, Maids-a-milking! Merry (almost) Christmas!

Just stopped in to make sure you're not slacking off now that Charlotte and I have graduated. Glad to see all your pump bags lined up and the notebook pages filled!

As for me, of course I'm still breastfeeding Charlotte. She's starting to refuse to nurse on my "milk dud" (right side). Its leaky sprinkler squirted her in the face one too many times. Now, whenever I try to put her on my right side, she says, "No! Side!" I called my lactation consultant and she said it's OK to let one side dry out. I didn't even know that was possible! Apparently, our breasts don't talk to each other about how much milk they're making, so one side can completely go dry while the other one continues producing. My right side was barely making milk anyway, so I hardly notice the difference. Except that now I'm even more lopsided than ever. Think I can find a hybrid bra??? You know, one side sexy and lacy, B cup; the other side thick cotton nursing bra, DD cup.

By the way, can you keep a secret? I mean it—you are sworn to secrecy! OK?

See the next page. . . .

You really can't tell anyone!!

I'm trusting you.

Promise????

I am **PREGNANT!!!!!** Hooray!!!

So far, only my parents, my sister, and my doctor know. And Chris, of course! And now, you. As a matter of fact, I just did a pregnancy test right *here* in the *IBM bathroom*!

IT'S POSITIVE!

+ +

(OK, it's my 3rd test. I just wanted to be sure because the + was so faint on the first two, so I stopped at Walgreens on my way to work today.)

Due date (according to the magic wheel) is August 18. I think we may have conceived on Charlotte's birthday! They'll be 21 months apart.

It's TOO GOOD TO BE TRUE!

Now . . . is it too much to ask for another redheaded girl??

Love, Cate

P.S. Shhhhhhhhhhhhhhhhhh. I mean it.

ANOTHER BUN IN THE OVEN?

Just when you've conquered getting the stroller collapsed and in the car, the diaper bag stocked and loaded, and your daughter sunscreened and buckled in her car seat, all in under five minutes, the question may arise: Are you ready for another baby? Suddenly you're captivated by every newborn you see, oohing and ahhing at their tiny hats, little hands in fists, and peaceful sleeping faces. Childbirth, fussiness, gas, and spit-up have miraculously faded into distant memory. Some friends tell you that having another baby is pretty much like carrying another purse, and you might as well do it now while your body is still in the flabby pregnancy mode and you're under forty. Others tell you that your body needs a break and that adding another child is like inviting an army into your home, increasing the chaos, cost, stress, and mess exponentially. Who's right? It depends.

 sibling spacing facts

- A two-year spacing is the national average in the United States.
- The U.S. Centers for Disease Control and Prevention (CDC) recommends conceiving a child eighteen to twenty-three months

after the birth of a previous baby. The CDC study found this sibling spacing interval provided for the greatest likelihood that the baby would be carried full term and have a healthy birth weight.

There are many advantages to welcoming another baby into your family within three years. You're still in baby mode—the changing table is still set up with a few size-one diapers on the shelf. Your electrical outlets are baby-proofed, glass vases are out of reach, and you have a cabinet full of bibs, bottles, and sippy cups. You've got a network of babysitters and friends, and you're on a first-name basis with the pediatritian and preschool teacher. Your maternity and baby clothes are still in style and not packed away in the basement yet. For many parents, the most compelling reason to have kids close together is that they'll grow to be natural playmates and companions. Although their personalities will differ, their interests will be close enough that they can happily romp at the park, play dress-up, read books, and watch *Sesame Street* together. Of course, having two kids under the age of three is overwhelming and exhausting, but most moms say that by the time the youngest is out of diapers, things start to click, making it all worthwhile. Another consideration is that the younger a child is when a new baby arrives, the less trouble he'll have adjusting to no longer being your one and only.

On the flip side, there are plenty of reasons to wait four or more years before getting pregnant again. For one, a longer interval between kids gives you more time and energy to devote to each baby/toddler during the years they need you most. This gives you the freedom to truly enjoy and get to know each little one. You'll have a chance to rediscover yourself (and your husband), read a novel or two, get to the gym, and wear your favorite jeans. As for your child, she'll have an opportunity to be a nurturer, leader, and role model for her baby brother. She'll be old enough to get herself dressed, get a snack out of the pantry, and go potty on her own, while you're busy nursing the baby and changing his diaper. Wider sibling spacing also has financial advantages: you can spread your expenses over several years, making day-care costs and college tuition easier to bear.

Whatever you decide, you can be sure that the degree of chaos and rivalry—or harmony and closeness—between children is not just the result of how close in age they are. The impact of sibling spacing on family dynamics depends largely on your temperament and that of your husband and children. Laid-back parents with an independent older child will probably have an easier time raising kids close in age than a highly structured family with a needy first child.

Another huge factor to consider is how adding another child will affect your career. Repeating the cycle of pregnancy, maternity leave, and pumping again (ugh) within a few years may slow your advancement. On the other hand, compressing the time you're in major mommy mode can enable you to plan and manage your career trajectory in phases. One Mama described phase one as the scenic route— a time primarily devoted to caring for her two children. She worked reduced hours, and remained in the same job for five years, forgoing a promotion. Once her kids started grade school, she began phase two, the business route. She returned to work full-time, but still carefully preserved her mommy time, attending school plays and ballet recitals and becoming a Girl Scout leader. In phase three, when her kids are in high school, she'll be ready for the autobahn—pedal to the metal again, taking her career wherever she wants it to go.

No matter how much you deliberate or agonize over the pros and cons of when to have another baby, life has a way of imposing itself upon your best-laid plans. You may get pregnant when you least expect it, or you and your partner may have sex like bunnies, with no results. Also, since many moms these days are having their first children at older ages, waiting several years to have another may not be a viable option. Try not to worry if life sneaks in and does the planning for you. Know that even when parents are able to plan the spacing of their kids, there's no crystal ball for telling how well siblings will get along or how they'll be affected emotionally and psychologically. The only thing parents can know for sure is that whenever they have another child, that child will be a blessing.

Monday, December 17

Congratulations, Cate! I am so happy for you and Chris! And Charlotte, too. She's going to be the best big sister. And I promise to keep your secret.

Can you believe my little guy will turn 1 next month?? I'm actually sorry to say that my pumping and nursing days are almost over. Never thought I'd feel this way. But he's losing interest, and I'm down to a trickle. At this point, I'm just milking the experience as long as I can, so to speak.

We miss you!

Andrea

Monday, December 17

YEA CATE!! That is GREAT news! How are you feeling?

Anne

Monday, December 17

Cate,

I am so glad to know that you will be back in this room next year encouraging other new IBM moms. (You are coming back to work, aren't you?!)

I know a woman in IBM Global Services who is about ready to pop. Her baby is due any day, and she's carrying a towel in her computer bag because she's sure her water is going to break in a conference room. I made her promise that she'll give pumping in our palace a go when she comes back in March.

Stacy

Tuesday, December 18

I have a friend who is coming back to work right after Christmas. She's definitely going to breastfeed and pump. I told her I'd bequeath my Pump In Style to her and show her the ropes. Imagine that—ME teaching someone else how to pump, and giving advice on how to juggle nursing and working and mothering without losing your head.

Andrea

COMING ATTRACTIONS

By now you know that working motherhood is a bit like having one foot in a roller skate at all times. So it will come as no surprise that even after you and your baby graduate from breastfeeding, the balancing act continues in all its glory. Despite your newfound freedom from nursing and pumping and your baby's increasing independence, there are new hurdles to overcome. Before you know it, you'll be juggling work, a two-year-old whose favorite word is "no," and the ins and outs (ha!) of potty training. One Mama told us she found pumping at work easy going compared to convincing her three-year-old daughter not to wear her pink Sleeping Beauty princess panties every day of the week. Clothing battles will soon be followed by the first day of kindergarten, school performances and fund-raisers, parent-teacher conferences, Girl/Boy Scouts, homework, and sporting events. You can also look forward to monthly orthodontist appointments (and bills), piano lessons, report card surprises, discipline issues, first loves, and last-minute errands to buy everything from birthday gifts to track shoes. The older your kids get, the more places you have to be at once. At times, you'll feel like an undertipped chauffeur and your house will seem like a hotel where your teenagers check in with a mumble, eat, sleep, change clothes, and leave again.

Even though they seem to need you less during this time, they actually need you every bit as much as they did when they were in diapers. As working moms, we'll always feel pulled between our children, our careers, and the rest of our lives. But simply surviving the baby years and forming lasting friendships with other working moms will prepare you well for the maze that lies ahead.

Tuesday, December 18

Hi, all.

Had to stop back in to see your reactions to my big news. Thanks for all your congrats. I knew you'd be excited! I'm feeling great, but VERY TIRED. Yes, I'll be back, but I'm going to ask for a 6-month leave, and I really want to come back part-time—3 or 4 days a week. Wish me luck.

I'm glad you're recruiting new Milk Mamas. I always do the same. I'm so nosy—whenever I see a pregnant woman at IBM, I tell her about our little club. My wish is that so many moms would pump at work that we would totally outgrow this room, and IBM would let us take over the huge executive conference room down the hall. We'd replace the giant oval table with comfy sofas.

Now, before I sign off I want to leave you all with these gifts: some fun-colored pens and three brand-new spiral notebooks. I'm expecting all the new Milk Mamas to make good use of them so that when I come back, needing support and a few good laughs, I'll have plenty to read. And more friends to count on.

Cate, XXOO

epilogue

HOW DID WE DO IT?

We battled sleep deprivation, lugged our pumps to and fro, found time during busy workdays to pump, cried because we missed our babies, second-guessed our work and child-care choices, worried about milk supply, and weathered bottle strikes and spills. Somehow, we persevered through it all, emerging more complete and stronger than we ever could have predicted. The whole experience was everything we'd heard it would be: overwhelming and exhausting. It was also surprisingly rewarding. During those unforgettable first days back at work, we entered the janitor closet/lactation room tired, sad, and filled with doubts, questions, and guilt. But somehow, by the time we hung our babies' pictures on the Graduate Wall, wrote farewell messages in the Milk Mama notebooks, and carried our pumps home for the last time, we were brimming with a sense of accomplishment, pride, and desire to help other new moms conquer the challenges we had overcome. We never expected that by the time our babies were toddlers we'd actually feel nostalgic about pumping breastmilk! It's not that we forgot how hard it was, but as with childbirth, our memories of the experience heighten its beauty and sweetness and diminish its difficulty. Like all moms, we love remembering when our babies fit like puzzle pieces on our hips, and nestled securely and peacefully at our breasts. While in a dull meeting or wading through a sea of e-mail, we even occasionally daydream about the moments spent in that lactation room, taking pause from IBM chaos to sit quietly, provide breastmilk for our babies, and cheer each other on. Who would have guessed that while IBM vice presidents were down the hall in cold, windowless conference rooms reviewing business results, making important decisions, and discussing deadlines and strategy, we Milk Mamas sat inside a closet turned pumping palace, pouring out raw emotion and a basic life source?

THE MILK MEMOS LESSON

We now know with certainty that juggling a full-time career, family, and all of life's other demands *is* possible (but not always easy or graceful). We doubted ourselves in the beginning, but learned that we each had the capacity to succeed all along—and so do you. It starts with day-by-day commitment, determination, courage, and a sense of humor. To go the distance, though, you need to look outside of yourself and connect with other working moms.

If you're nursing, create your own Milk Mama circle in your workplace, local community, or online. Like us, you will meet moms who love to breastfeed and others who dutifully endure it. You'll find babies who love to nurse, and others who need convincing. There will be moms who thrive on pumping at work, and some who can't stand it. Some women will dream of staying at home full-time; others will enjoy the balance of working outside and inside the home. Some will be determined to give their babies nothing but breastmilk; others will use formula without thinking twice. No matter the viewpoints you encounter, you'll be united by a common desire to give breastfeeding while working a try. In the end, you'll help each other succeed, whether that means breastfeeding for a year or managing to pump for a couple months after returning to work. And we promise, one day you will find yourself looking back with pride and fondness on the whole crazy experience.

THE MILK MEMOS DREAM

We hope that in *The Milk Memos* you have found practical advice, humor, support, encouragement, and the confidence that you *can* combine motherhood, breastfeeding, and career. Share your success with coworkers, sisters, relatives, and friends. Your story will inspire the next mom, and hers will inspire the next. One by one, we will contribute to a culture in which achieving a satisfying work-life balance is possible for most working parents, and returning to work is no longer the chief reason women stop breastfeeding.

For this to be possible, we must go beyond encouraging and supporting each other. It is incumbent upon each of us to demand that our employers do more in support of parents. With conviction and persistence, together we will make a difference, pushing employers to *really* deliver access to flexible work options without penalizing employees who utilize them. To boost breastfeeding rates, we must call on employers to provide the support, time, and space for pumping breastmilk. We look forward to the day when every workplace treats parents, especially nursing moms, with the respect and support they deserve. Let this new image be the only workplace our children will ever know.

THE MILK MAMAS TODAY

Cate gave birth to another healthy, beautiful baby girl, Mary, and then took a well-deserved six-month maternity leave. While still pregnant, she continued nursing Charlotte for six months, then rested her breasts for three months, and went on to nurse Mary for over two years. Cate went back to work at IBM, and found that returning the second time was every bit as hard as the first. Tears still flowed, guilt crept in, and she struggled daily with the transition between patty-cake Mommy and strategic-planning Manager. But this time around, she had the benefit of experience and knew she could mix a baby (and a toddler) with business. Through the journals, she continued to help other new moms do the same. Cate eventually pared her workweek down to four days, taking Fridays off to write this book and spend time with her girls. Later, Cate returned to a full-time workweek, and is now a marketing program manager for IBM. At time of publication, Charlotte is five and Mary is three.

Andrea wrote her last entry in the journals when Caleb was eleven months. She is forever grateful to the Milk Mamas for helping her through those unforgettably difficult months, and inspiring her to pump more than twice as long as she had planned. Had she known in the beginning what she learned through the notebooks about buying the right pump, boosting supply, and nursing in general, she's sure she could have completed a full year. But with her milk drying up and Caleb losing interest, she reached her last nursing date, just shy of Caleb's first birthday. On that last day, she closed the door to Caleb's room, picked him up, sat in their favorite rocking chair, and nursed as she closed her eyes and etched the moment to memory, still surprised at how much she had grown to love nursing and how much she would miss it. At IBM, after months of negotiations, Andrea finally moved to a three-day workweek. She continues to work part-time as an internal and field communications specialist. At time of publication, Caleb is four, Cody, fourteen, and Sierra, eleven.

Cate and Andrea actively participate in workshops at IBM and elsewhere encouraging working moms to continue nursing and to support each other. Both are indebted to all the Milk Mamas who contributed to the original notebooks, and who became the personalities of Stacy, Anne, Stephanie, and Samantha.

The Pumping Palace is still in use today. As you read this, pump bags are waiting on the same old brown medical table, parts are drying on racks, and babies' faces are lining the Graduate Wall alongside Charlotte and Caleb.

appendix

Many Milk Mamas find it helpful to keep track of how much milk they produce at each pumping session and/or how much milk their babies drink at day care. The following logs may be useful for this purpose.

We know firsthand that some Milk Mamas obsess about these details, especially in the beginning. Try to relax and trust Mother Nature to work her breastfeeding supply-and-demand magic. Although not instantaneously, your body *will* respond to your baby's appetite—we promise. And your baby will not starve!

Please visit www.milkmemos.com, where you'll find these logs plus many other resources.

Milk Mama Production Log

Day	Date	FIRST PUMPING SESSION				SECOND PUMPING SESSION				Daily Total	Comments
		Time	Left Side	Right Side	Total	Time	Left Side	Right Side	Total		
			oz.	oz.	oz.		oz.	oz.	oz.	oz.	

Note: This and other breastmilk production logs (e.g., for tracking three pumping sessions per day) are available online at milkmemos.com

Look How Much Milk I Drank, Mommy!

Sample Day-Care Provider Breastmilk Intake Log

Day/Date	Time	SERVED				TOTAL		LEFTOVERS		Comments
		Fresh	Reused	Frozen	Formula	Offered	Finished	Saved	Discarded	
			(amount of each)			(amount of each)		(check one)		
		oz.	oz.	oz.	oz.	oz.	oz.			

Note: This and log, and variations on it, are available online at milkmemos.com

acknowledgments

Although we can't get past feeling that we're living a dream, we want to thank the following people for helping to make this book a reality:

To Laura Berman Fortgang and *Redbook* magazine, who lit a fire under us after we had pondered our idea for three years. Laura, you showed us how it was possible to work an IBM job, run a household, write a book, and emerge with marriages and sanity intact.

To our agent, Stephanie Kip Rostan, who pumped milk for her son Luke in the old fur vault. We have been blessed by your understanding, humor, support, responsiveness, and ideas. And to Jim Levine, the first (male) honorary Milk Mama.

To our editor, Sara Carder, who we now know read our manuscript with an extra-discerning eye, having just found out that she was going to be a Milk Mama herself. Thank you for your unbridled enthusiasm and insightful editing.

To our lactation consultants: Darcy Kamin, who also helped Cate succeed at breastfeeding and appreciate its beauty, and Amanda Ogden, whose fine-toothed comb and extensive knowledge helped us arm Milk Mamas with the latest and most essential ideas and facts.

To Milk Mamas at IBM and elsewhere who shared their stories with us.

To Kreighton Beiger, who came up with the title.

To Orbit Bubblemint gum, chai tea, strong coffee, and local libraries, cafes, and bookstores.

To IBM, for providing the room that became our pumping palace—and for establishing family-friendly policies, inspiring other companies to do the same, and helping pave the way for progress yet to come. Thank you to our managers, mentors, and colleagues who supported our dream and provided the flexibility we needed.

To the babysitters, nannies, and au pairs who lovingly cared for our children as we worked on the book.

From Andrea

To Roger, who always believed, never discouraged, and willingly helped me find time to write. Thank you for your constancy, optimism, and for "writing the middle" with me. You are THE one. ICLU.

To Caleb, Cody, and Sierra, for your silliness and for showing me how immense my capacity is for love.

To my parents, Rick and JoAnne Morgan, for your enthusiasm, support, interest, and love—and the incredible book cake!

To Marcia O'Neal, for being the angel you are. You—and your cooking—nourish me.

To Chad, for your creativity and for love without strings. Can I please have your brownie now?

To Cate, my FCA, my for-a-lifetime friend. Your Excel skills astound, your H&M looks amaze, your zest for pinks, greens, and funky prints bring cheer, and your smarts, compassion, sensitivity, and heart inspire. I couldn't have done this alone.

From Cate

To Chris, for lifting me up when I needed it most, and for being calm, dependable, strong, funny, romantic, and devoted. I love you.

To Charlotte and Mary, for being yourselves, thereby helping me find myself.

To my parents, Frank and Charlotte Colburn, for your constant love, unfailing support, and incomparable generosity—and for teaching me to pass it on.

To Anne Colburn Ehrhart, for being an inspiration and beacon in so many ways. To Mark Colburn, for more than redeeming yourself after becoming mean on your eleventh birthday.

To Andrea, for sharing the dream, for never giving up despite burnt pizza and a fire that fizzled, for being brilliant, and for being my kindred spirit and friend for life.

A special toast to Lily Chin, Brenda Colburn, Katie Doran, Meghan Earthman, Debra Fitzgibbons, Heather Ford, Matt Graber, Stacy Hayes Graber, Hugh Hartshorne, Laura Ingman, Kristin Johnson,

Jenny Kabakovich, Kat Kimball, Hilde Kraiss, Cam Low, Alice Cook Madison, Eve McCormick, Shelly Miller, Jackie Price, Kate Rogers, Susan Rosewell-Jackson, Nea Sullivan, Catherine Tallerico, and the many others whose time, support, and encouragement made it all possible.

And most of all, to God, whose plans for us are larger than we could ever imagine, and who will lead us onward to our next great adventure.

index

about the authors

Cate Colburn-Smith was raised in Tulsa, Oklahoma, and has called Boulder, Colorado, home since attending the University of Colorado, where she earned a B.S. in business. In seventeen years at IBM, she has worked in marketing, strategy, sales, and management positions. Successful but never quite fulfilled in corporate high-tech, Cate spent the better part of her twenties and thirties longing to discover her true passion. Then she found motherhood, breast-feeding, and writing—and through *The Milk Memos*, the chance to combine all three, plus her business experience, into a crusade with purpose. Cate loves a good snow storm, a lazy morning, coffee with cream, her mellow dog and two purring cats, her cruiser bike, long hugs from her husband, and elaborate make-believe games with her two beautiful daughters.

Andrea Serrette was born and raised in Boulder, Colorado and earned bachelor's and master's degrees in English and journalism from the University of Colorado. She is still addicted to the Rocky Mountains and lives in Boulder, where she writes internal and executive communications for a division within IBM and helps manage three kids, two nutty dogs, and one really tenacious fish—as well as orthodontist appointments and volleyball, soccer, and cross-country schedules. When she's not busy (ha!) with these things, she can be found riding her bike, running, reading books with her husband, playing dominoes with the kids, or slurping a banana milk shake. Before dreaming up the idea to turn the lactation room journals into a book, she wondered what she was put on this earth to do. Now she knows.

For Milk Mama references and resources, visit
www.milkmemos.com